FROM ALMOST EVERYWHERE

FROM ALMOST EVERYWHERE

FRANCO BELTRAMETTI

SELECTED POEMS
1965-1995

EDITED BY *Stefan Hyner*

FONDAZIONE FRANCO BELTRAMETTI
& BLACKBERRY BOOKS
2016

Copyright © 2016 by
the heirs to the literary and artistic estate of Franco Beltrametti

Copyright © 2016 for this edition by
Blackberry Books, Nobleboro, Maine

for the translations of *Another Earthquake*
Copyright © 1974, 1976 by Paul Vangelisti
(*Un altro terremoto* originally published 1971
by Edizioni Geiger, Torino, Italy)

Copyright © 2011 for the epilogue by Stefan Hyner

Cover image: Franco Beltrametti, ink on paper
GATE magazine #5, 1996

Photographs: *page 130* / by Antonio Ria (Raworth & Beltrametti)
page 136 / by Lloyd Kahn (Beltrametti house)
page 166 / by Antonio Ria (Beltrametti reading)
back cover: Franco & Giona Beltrametti by Judy Dancinger

Book design: JB Bryan / La Alameda Press

Set in Bembo & Arrighi

ISBN: 978-09824389-8-5

All Rights Reserved

Blackberry Books
617 East Neck Road
Nobleboro, ME 04555
chimfarm@gwi.net

CONTENTS

Editor's Note / *9*

Books
    Face to Face / *13*
    One of Those Condor People / *41*
    Another Earthquake / *71*
    Airmail Postcards / *83*
    Target / *95*
    The X Book / *109*
    Surprise / *115*
    Three For Nado / *131*
    California Totem / *137*

Paintings / *167*

Broadsides & Concertina Books / *177*

Miscellaneous Poems / *185*

Recent Work 1994-1995 / *225*

F.B. Talks Poetry / *229*

Epilogue / *247*

Bibliography / *257*

EDITOR'S NOTE

"English is not my native language,
but language is not my native speech."
Franco Beltrametti

This selection contains all poems of Franco Beltrametti, either written in English originally or translated, that were published during his lifetime as independent books or in magazines and anthologies. The only exceptions are the poems in Recent Work 1994-1995, which were taken from the manuscript Beltrametti was working on at the time of his death in the fall of 1995.

With the exception of frequent compound nouns, most of the spelling peculiarities in these poems derive from Jaime de Angulo's phonetic spelling of the English language, which Beltrametti adopted early on without dogmatically forcing the issue. At the risk of confusing the reader at first, we have kept the way the poems were originally published, while obvious typos and/or misspellings were silently corrected. Every attempt was made to have the poem appear on the page as Franco had arranged them in the previous publications, which also meant keeping the variations in dating. Only in *Another Earthquake* are the poems dated in the American fashion — that is, the month before the day — quite possibly a decision of the translator Paul Vangelisti.

With the exception of a rare number of individual poems in magazines and anthologies Beltrametti translated his own work, with the help of a native speaker such as Judy Danciger or James Koller; *Another Earthquake* is the sole exception. Late in his life it seems that Beltrametti wrote many of the poems directly in English; there are often no versions of those poems in any other language among his papers.

The manuscript for this book was arranged as follows: first, all books, chapbooks, and broadsides in order of their publication dates; second, the

English poems from books that also contain poems in other languages; third, poems from anthologies and magazines not included in any of the above; and, finally, poems from collaborations with other authors that are clearly marked as written by Franco Beltrametti.

This book could not have been realized without the help of a number of people. I want to thank Franca and Giona Beltrametti for their support throughout the duration of the project. Thanks to Anna Ruchat of the Fondazione Franco Beltrametti for her tireless work securing the finances. I am especially thankful to Joanne Kyger for her encouragement from the outset and for proofing the manuscript, as did Bobby Byrd, Donald Guravich, Rita Degli Esposti and John Gian, thanks to you all. My gratitude also goes to Maggie Brown for editing the epilogue and to JB Bryan for his meticulous work designing the book.

And finally, as always, to Marianne Steele, who kept the home fire burning and bandaged the wounded.

FACE TO FACE

FOR JAMES KOLLER

My demons
I see coming out
even from where
I thought them exorcised
— they say they're feeling well
— we're getting to be friends

14/12/70

A NOTE FOR GARY SNYDER

(the music I heard
wasnt music
and I carry around
the weight of many
ghosts (rumor for instance
       a humidifier
(right at my back
face to face

    "a few inches of snow outside
melting, now"

23/1/73

, yes, realizing Shirakawa each
              moment was the aim (the white
river "would flow in one ear
         & out the other" / something else
realizing thunderbird (a
            ballpoint pen
     (that racket
         could be the gagaku
of millions of insects gone

13/11/71
for Philip Whalen

(SHORT REPORT) : (TOWARDS NOVEMBER)

at the intersection of the 107th latitude
with the 27th longitude synchronize
the calendars' nodes

with botanical spirals on face & ankles
& pupils cerebral barometers dilated
we'll come back alive

to see ourselves planets & suns on the invariable
itinerary / the absolute fixity of halts
lets you follow us

stage on stage the upland plain offers stones
as pillows recalling analogous
journeys of no return

15/11/71

in spite of the first snow violent wind
in spite of the dry lake imaginary fish
in spite of the evening burnt wood smell
in spite of the "what's the use of trying"
        the "I can't help it"
in spite of the rigmarole of
in spite ofs

20/11/71

        in
        a
        wink
nothing but the truth:
        sitting (rain
                outside) in the cold
    on a black bear skin
            ALL
                      I SEE
                IS ROCK
    ALL
      I HEAR
    IS WIND

21/1/72

the journey has poles
(intentions, on the way
under the skin)
the parking unlimited
(without pretenses
    IF TRUCKS HAD
DREAMS & MEMORIES
???
??
?

25/1/72

THE KEY

> What was well started shall be finished.
> What was not, should be thrown away.
> Lew Welch, from *Hermit Poems*

1) The place & the season : winter
2) somebody (myself) right here : real & unreal
3) what is he doing & what's going on in his head
4) how & why is he saying it
5) to somebody else (you) elsewhere
   something happens?
   the circle (real & unreal)
   isnt closed

27/1/72

RABELAISIAN LETTER
TO ADRIANO SPATOLA
MULINO DI BAZZANO

lets play chess again, the pawns logs of
sequoia gigantea
the king a dwarf pine
a pint of whisky
each move not exceed 250 years
panim sukum sukdavi, tobacco smoke (in Maidu)
drifting—
I am not immune : in the diggin's (I dreamed)
gold was left, 30-40 cm spangles
I traded for boots & a sheep skin vest
the last grizzly bear was seen in 1924
plenty of black ones
between 1200 & 8500 feet

29/1/72
Sierra Nevada

I SAW THE
GREEN YUBA RIVER
FLOW

         (following under manzanita
a clear sheer
deer & coyote path
      beyond the rocks where the Maidu
      people for centuries ground acorns
in perfect mortars hollowed by use
in granite

      (diving in dizzy perspectives
opening
hawks
         on the sinuous dancing blue pines
among the
yellow

    I saw the Yuba river
flow
      green winding down single rapid
      angular shining
      boulders

& finally understood
what it means to

flow
    without
        edges

8/2/72

THE WIND IN THE PINES
BOW ARROW EYE TARGET
ETC.

                        a series of irresistible waves
                        from all directions
                        in all directions

(nothing
is really changed . . .

9/2/72

QUAND LES FEUX DU DÉSERT S'ÉTAIGNENT UN À UN
— Pierre Reverdy

"to make it explicit"
or
"to take off the lid"
only to discover other (apparent)
        lids
        or
        situations
        1,2,3 rainbows

11/2/72

>   *. . . he valued what's clean & succinct*
> *washing in a cold stream his stone tooth . . .*
>   Ou-yang Hsiu
>   S<small>UNG</small> D<small>YNASTY</small>

                for James Koller in the snow
                          1500 miles to the east
     (from the window crowded with moths)
have you got gun knife
flashlight?
        then we can go
& went
              (((Hsiu had a strange hat
                  a long beard
                    & rejected obsessive melancholy)))
              (((pure
                 fantasy)))
I dont have the gun
the rest yes
& we went
              anyway

16/2/72

but then you really dont get it :
the water under the bridge
rushing — they call it
river
                      the stone house
is the bears' — they bite glasses —
deer with grass
grow wings & too late
the trap snaps (& you
then
        really dont
            get it
                                      while
we're
gone

27/5/72

To force limits a fixed rule.
Impossible
to put off. Steal
from night from day.　　Kill
flags.　Comrades got busted, didnt shine
shoes. Respect
the stranger passing.
3 trees clouds rocks a meadow.
Another perspective saying
beat it

19/6/72

Dont lose even a
minute. Relentless facts.　I greet you.
In the wall a walled-up arch.
In spite of the sticks pumpkins
didnt grow.
Sure mist.　The moon has a halo.
What a combination.
The picture, you say, thrown into the void.
Thought, dictated, out of control.
Sure that naked you
are beautiful.　You can say this.　Between
simultaneous firmaments.

21/6/72

Consider
                    how far
the push
                    carries
you.
                    Be surprised at the wall
the silence. Get
beyond
the echo
of what
it is
has been.

23/6/72

WAY UP
for Giorgio Mariani

        I cut with my knife a clear light
crystal. Half
jumps
gets lost
on granite   slabs. Soon
substituted for by
fire's flower. Not even an eye (you say)
      of open sky. I see (you say) mountains
        making themselves. Without cups spoons, how
        would we manage (I say). The night
        never arrives — smoke smoke
                smoke
                    thru the roof — says
who.

29/6/72

It goes even if badly   :   the toothed
spoon slaughtering insects
& meadow grass.
It wasnt dawn the leprous moon — we're
stuck. It's good
the staff
                    Jaguar / Horse / Deer.
Shake pumpkin rattle.
Stretch the iron drum's skin
starry robe.
Strong your heart, fire & water.
Flutter wings
give handful of earthy
smoke.

5/7/72
for Ben Eagle

RAMIFICATIONS

     Ready
         for the appearance
         of tracks to
         follow —
         for the allusion
of junctions with no indications
                       (((because you really
exist : with zigzag lightnings in your hands
        with furs on your shoulders
        among glass chips
sparks)))
         to the heights of dreams the
         hunt for
         signs

7/8/72
PARTANNA

BROKEN FLIGHTS
(VISION, WINDS, DUST)

      Crossed on the ferry
for the seventh time the strait. Hit by
winds of forgotten
dust. Palma da Montechiaro
hallucination of the spirit.
Veils flutter on scattered brides spread out
among

      cut off columns. Out of cities in spreading
ruins. Landslides hung to
red cliffs. Damnation of
levels on the highway
ramps. Stolen
earth.

      Rare silence roars. Pentagonal wasps'
nests. Round quarries. The volcano not
far. Circular saw screech
cutting tufa. Why

      on earth this
poison. Green yellow lights.
Dazzling.

      Nights under bats' broken flights
intercepted by fixed
lights. Here we
lived.

11/8/72
Lu Pisciu, Western Sicily

FOR ORION IN MID AUTUMN

1

       Orion,
             shoulders belt knees
    rises diagonally :   not cloud
banks those but (space) walls of
      rock.
                    (((Hypothesis :   walk sitting in the game
of parentheses. The simplest thoughts.
                  Long evenings passed. You :   out of the
    seashell. Memories' acute angles. Intelligence
of straw. Brushfires.)))
    Think it over — along rows of persimmons
in line. Orion
glides.   He-of-the-belt. On the
mountain. Seven sisters
on the riversides.
Were you looking for (space) someone.

2

    Orion, him again, on the ridge (((no, it was the
halo of the white moon close to the chimney, and rocks.
I say, and clouds,
too))). Bet
    with yourself — see where you
end up. Remember
the fire the flames the
smoke the
rest.

3

      Orion, the mountain behind which it rises, all the
rest — are
and are not here.
      What's left is a great desire to grasp them
for what we are — us and them — hanging
from the same thread. They have voices, we
heard them, they said
this.

15/11/72

FOR A CAMPHOR TREE (ON AN ISLAND IN ANOTHER CONTINENT)

1

You say, now (it's a bet)
it's all going
to hell.　　Whatever it is.
　　　　　　Wherever it goes.
　　　　　　It seems to be the tendency.
　　　　　　That only
　　　in 1000 years or 17 seconds could be
reversed — minimal condition
for not having to move from under
a camphor tree.

2

　　　　　　Embers become
fire, introspection creaks like stretched
　　　　leather, gaudy and plain, at half past
　　　　　　midnight 50 km out of town.
　　　　　　Eating tangerines.
　　　　Missing people — lots.

3

　　　　　　Once we took
　　　　too much of something,
whatever it was.　Since the we stayed
　　　　there — reasoning this way, moving
　　　　　　only in this territory.

23/12/72

        Because it is the violent red
framing a diamond of blue and green threads
while the recordplayer croaks
while the Pacific shells shine
cold on the white walls.
                        Sure
there are
better times (thin walls creak, doors
slam). What counts in here   :
a lamp. You wouldnt
believe it.

10/1/73

AFTER YOU GET IT : FORGET IT

        History doesnt always tell lies!
François Villon, never met?
I never set foot
on Easter Island!
Krazy Kat comes in goes out the window!
I dont every day use exclamation marks!
Searching for a new project
every morning I expect a renewed
world — a new fact!
Within the given span of time
an arrow : the unforeseen!

3/2/73
for Claude Pélieu

The words that the desert says
arent the words that the desert says
but those that people say
thinking or living the desert
attributing him a language
and opinions, yet never proved
never the same — seen as each one
carries with (inside & outside) his own
desert (or seas, or glacier)
made to measure. Confronted
with a real desert (Mohave, Painted
Desert) one discovers
that he is or could be a
person — another person —
than the one taken for granted (even
the most unrestrained perceptive
imagination
is dumbfounded.

30/1/73

THE BIG QUARTER OF AN HOUR

      "A trail only for birds" : the precision
of old Tu Fu strikes
at distance. Here comes the rising sun
the courtyard lights up.
Mountains to the east / mountains to the west.
      (I gave myself a quarter of an hour : it's past.

6/2/73

in Venice at the Giudecca
    (from the low water under the wooden bridge
metal wreckage surfaces)
I think of the Caffè Trieste in San Francisco
and of the wineshop all'Antica Mormorazione
in Trieste
where yesterday
I was thinking of Venice
at the Giudecca

7/3/73

ANALOGOUS POEM
23/3/73

    Here I'm air meat & bones as a way of saying it passing
from the blackest despair
to the pungent drug of euphoria

    This is right this is wrong are words
of the wounded beast — but I keep to each analogy

    I'm 36 I discover waking up still feeling
the warm imprint of your hand at the end of the dream

    We went up we came down — you are smooth
as an undulant field with rocks floating below

    I was your favorite and you were mine — long legs
eyes able to open wide to your vision
of big animal not willing to disappear

    In the impossible reservation you
exiled yourself on your own and I with you — come what may
figure that this is what there is

    A poem of love keeps intact its nakedness
from beginning of world — whether on sand or grass

    Which polluted water should I bring
to the mill of malfunctioning — what isnt said is here
highways factories jails vast stations

    How do you expect me to wait for their slow erosion
to kiss you

★ ★
★

"IN THE DARK TAVERN OF OUR BIRTH"

.... the sun can shine as long as it wants
the quietness at center that can "take" every
tempest : a continual wreck! I'm no
exception : I dont understand myself as I dont understand you
him the others. I draw a tangent
that may carry me away : of
my poems they will say : clear as lightning.
Only me I wont have understood
even that.

29/3/73

reckonings dont come even
roughly on the same latitude as
Sevilla / Richmond / Wichita / Nigata /
       Seoul / Askhabad
magpies
      from one carob tree
to the next

10/7/70

ONE OF THOSE
CONDOR PEOPLE

from: TRANS-SIBERIAN RAILWAY
   for Judy she Rimbaud

1. it was the victory parade
   a crowd around Red Square
   in the Café de l'Amitie
   I put together quickly
   the bundle of clothes & books
   the white smooth greek stone
   the alabaster pocket sculpture
   wound in a sock
   S.J. Perse Anabase
   the passport in a backpocket
   with the letter from Li Yen

9. run run run
   transsiberian train
   on the Shilka big ice slabs
   diagonally broken by thaw.
   those round brown hills
   I already know   (blue eyes my garden)
   from somewhere

14. Lenin Pushkin Dostojevski ghost Majakovskij
    saints painted blue
    outside the amusement park
    high on river Amur
    those distant mountains
    are Manchuria & China
    a band plays sprightly
    a little out of tune
    the wind brings the song

down to the riverbank
tomorrow from Khabarovsk to Nakhovka
only two days by sea
from Japan

19/5/65

TSUGARU KAIKYO

waking up
something creaks
rolling cabin
from the port
in the fog
far blue mountains
file past.
          — is this Japan?
a gulp of water, quickly
up on the wet deck
cool dawn wind

20/5/65

POEM BEGINNING WITH THE BEGINNING OF A POEM BY GARY SNYDER
for Ali Akbar Khan

THE TRUTH LIKE THE BELLY
OF A WOMAN TURNING — & lies?
Name the black & you have the strike of
the white
(sweet & sour is no solution).
Beautiful, I imagine : if one doesn't rush
truth
doesn't concern him anymore.
Everything is actually
up in the air — the bellybottom
ah yes! turns & turns
★ ★ ★ ★ ★ ★
★ ★ ★ ★ ★
★ ★ ★ ★
★ ★ ★
★ ★
★

WHITE ON BLACK :
wood & coal & rabbits, for sale

I think of the
good blonde she neighbor,
a strange hoarse voice.
Gone to Alaska.
Must
be cold,
now,
up there.

THE PERSIANS KNEW

from the asphalt road green walls shine in
darkness,
see thru a dry pepper tree
white ghost.
Inside
    sitting
        quietly
crosslegged
          in the cold evening
    wondering
what does
fly, if not me,   this
flying
carpet

A blown down
pine branch —
master Fo Yin & Su Tung Po
wrote the fallen-down-pine-branch
lamentation.
2 o'clock night
North Chorro Street
the kitchen windowglass
          went in a thousand pieces.
More air & wind
come in.

A BIRD?   AN EAGLE?

if you don't mind it seems to me a condor
Gymnogyps californianus,
almost extinct
(says the birds field identification guide)
a condor, seen with indian eye:
<u>One of those</u>
<u>condor</u>
<u>people</u>

?/1/1968

SUWANOSE JIMA *(for Nanao Sakaki)*
LAT. 29° 36'

Jaki jima : burning island.
Mist on the volcano, clouds, cool air after the
Typhoon.
Morning : two groups : the first
finishing the bamboo roundhouse
strawroof
        the second breaking sweet potato fields.
We decide to build a platform
up in the banyan tree flying off the cliff.
A revolution based on brown rice.
Sonoyama gives us a 3 month old goat
her place : on black lava
zen rock
her name : Lara.
Afternoon cutting bamboos.
Like the Sixth Patriarch. A clean blow.
Learning
I cut my knee.

26/7/67

TOSHIMA MARU
for Tetsuo Nagasawa & Pon Yamada

the ten islands boat
back & forth
back & forth
flying fish jump up
thru floating watermelon seeds
250 naked tons / diesel motor
Nakano jima seaside free hotspring
I leave too soon.

PHOTO BY A.L. KROEBER

— low Klamath river valley
   Yurok people
— from a redwood log
   a perfect shiny black
   dug out canoe
— skilled
   salmon trap builders
— in three pitches houses
— with beats as
   ancestors   as lovers

L.A. WATTS TOWERS ANTENNAE

Old Coyote was sleeping in the hills.
Old Coyote was sleeping in his house.
His house was back in the back of the hills.
In a little valley, in a hidden valley away back in the hills.
    Jaime de Angulo

Like Simon Rodia's 33 years of work
I'd like to build
a n-dimensional toy.
Yet I'm happy
caressing a Mount Tamalpais serpentine rock
or read in the sun
under the dead pepper tree
under the eucalyptus row
receiving friends
writing to them
frying eggplants
with rice
& salted plums

NAKASENDO
ROUTE 19   *for Giona*

                there:
rapids   foam   pools
        in white   boulders
       white rocks
there's the world   as I like it

   forests
& forests   mountains
  wooden villages
  sawmills

ricefields
   hitchhiking
on trucks
     down long the Kiso river

13/6/67
(((ON THE WAY BACK FROM FUJIMI
   ON THE WAY BACK TO KYOTO)))

Hey, what you think you doing
cutting down that tree?!
>   *for James Koller, the Driver*

If in a truck
a green pickup, on red steel
Golden Gate Bridge.
Why, is there a reason, this
sunny day — the bay all shining water —
why are your friends worried
or act like worriers to end up in
real worries?
Don't they know it's a
revolution?
Clear Mountain, let's go pray to the
Redwood Goddess
& take it
easy.

SAN LUIS OBISPO RAILWAY STATION
for my father, Gion

first morning coffee
people talk of that L.A. bum
who refused a 90, 000$ win
saying he didn't want
that kind of shit — I often go
                            to the railway station
to see rare trains
high palms & listen

DTM BROTHERHOOD FLASH
for Albert Saijo

    (OK, I'm glad to be here)

sometimes it's difficult to face
— supposing & even knowing
that table cups books lamps
all we see & don't
this house we are in
this very earth
my love my son, you and all of us
will vanish & go
to hell.   let's have
        more cups
        of tea.
    If all this is true
    that's me
    that's you   quietly
gone
      away

(((north of Klamath river)))

I CALL MY MEDICINE
WHITE DEER MY POISON
SHE ALWAYS COMES BACK
SOMETIMES MORE
SOMETIMES LESS

IT'S★GOING★BETTER★ALL★THE★TIME
for the 34 Evergreen Free Stone Peach Society

A Sung Dynasty landscape

    (in reality

a fossilized fern, casted black

on yellow sandstone.

        As big as my hand.

Older than mind — if any)

The stone from Baja

California you said.

53 SPARKES RD., SEBASTOPOL

After all this rain must be 1 o'clock night
Jim is back in the small white smoky room.
Real claws & feathers by a Durer's owl etching.
Wind & dogs howling again.
He pours more red wine. Are you hungry? he says.

29/12/67
for James Koller

look look
look at the killers crooked smiles
look how they got El Che
pierced his chest
many times
did him in for good
I don't understand but one thing is
clear:
      they won't cut him off
from us
& us
will bring him
back

?/?/1967
for Che Guevara

Bank of America College Square, San Luis Obispo
20.45 nobody around

JERRY MALONE PRODUCTION INC.
presents
LITTLE IRVY
20 tons   38 feet
---

a whale in a truck
frozen on two rails
35 cents to enter
see oncle Americo the misfit killed 1933
         in Santa Maria, California
ten seconds & out
in the chilly January night
shiny cars slide on
highway one

       I'M NO MORE A CIVILIZED MAN

SOME NEWS FROM LAOS
for Chuck Dockham

we spy (like kids) thru the door:
a kitchen like a highway
luminous
      crude
         chemical blue green —
all the rest
           a hermitage of electric candles:
burning —
I get high
only
entering

Discovered in a Thrifty Supermarket
a book: JOIN THE ARMY
& if you make it to become a general
& if you are good bombing napalm on Viet Nam
you'll make 1700 bucks a month
& more if you got some kind of family.
Going out I'm the only walker
on gas rainbow wet asphalt.
You can laugh at me:
my coat is waterproof & dirty, you
fools.

for Harry Hoogstraten who dated his letter
"another timeless dayless day if you don't
mind"

                A new switchblade knife,
                the handle brass & hard wood
                in my left pocket.
                A hand, two keys I don't really need
                in my right pocket.
                Reading your Rabelais Amsterdam Tales
                laughing
                hiking on Southern Pacific Railway
                level

from tie to tie.

TARATI ITI TARA (cleaning the ashes of a fire)

for a warlock girl

The tree-girl is standing, smooth nude body
wearing a necklace of brown seeds & indian corn.
Maybe smiling.
Her feet in the pentagonal terraces of the city
in red bricks & volcanic honey stone.
You can see the alembics thru the crystal-windows.
Fields mountains rocks on both sides
of the valley.
Eucalyptus windows.
Birds gliding higher than peaks
rapidly up &
slowly but slowly
down. Under the girl branches
right & left
sun & moon.
On her head a motionless hawk.
Her roots go thru the whole city.
Climbing up walls.
The city resting on the ground.
I wait. & then   pointing at the mountains she says
MOUNTAINS. I went away with her.
All this was long ago.   Maybe
now. Smooth bark / skin.

31/12/67
SAN FRANCISCO

★
there is nothing special to understand
just pay attention
★

11/3/69

> I want air in the evening & wine &
> chestnuts with friends
> Rocco Scotellaro

"My story tonight is that
the world is all the same
no borderlines of the earth
no borderlines of the mind.
Mountains / rivers / people
pass thru.
Body / speech / mind.
Bums are travelers, don't stay too long.
Today we've seen
the meadows greener & greener.
Magnolias almond plum peach trees blooming.
Highways are an imperfect
— useless —
attempt. All over California
spring dissolves asphalt & concrete
forever."

12/2/68
for Stefan

MESSAGE
From the lunatic people to whom it may concern.

—   unusual relations
  are usual
   for unusual people
      (what he means, what he means)
—   from A to Z
   from + to —
   from light to dark
      (what you mean what you mean)
—   two worlds
   back & forth from the sound
   barriers
   : a key

HANASHI
for Cid Corman & Kim Lawrence
23/5/67

hard to say what's the point
life & all of it
work done & not
days & nights, faces
years & places —
        more stars in us
than in this
        starry
         sky
          !

Indian oaks — peyote
the east slope of the mountain
covered with prickly pears

           the mountain the first volcano
the sixth is undersea
       out of Morro Rock
granite rock

by truck on one of the five roads
all this won't interest any of you
not even me
     only
  scrub oaks

(for Philip Whalen)

A broken necklace
— beads hard to find
in a parking lot.

Responsibility for errors
& autoindulgence of others
gratefully declined. From when
the mask is gone.

Consider yourself on yr. own: you
have it.

(for Judy)

(Adriano : fact is we are more than three millions
in a few square miles

birds : a few   condors : none
what a discovery after 30 days   the heat

the cold   the salty

a wooden silver insect
posed
          on raked sand   white sand
gravel)
          (one wins only not
playing?
etc.)
          (go away) (south) (to Partanna, Sicily)

---

for Adriano Spatola   10/7/69 Trastevere, Rome

ANOTHER EARTHQUAKE

To the comrades of Belice

1. imagine: incurable! a precise
   sensation (not unpleasant — not pleasing)
                 that everything is happening somewhere else
   at the speed of light SVAAAM   while here
   24 hours in a bolt of lightning of 6 months it was
                                        the twisting road
   up and down across the valley

3/31/70

4. ? are you — seeking — something — in — hiding?

this is too much. where did you
find it. who gave it
to you. where did it
end.

or else :
like tripping a
centipede ! ! ! ! ! ! ! ! ! ! ! ! ! ! ! ! ! !

(a false step
is not permitted)   3/28/70

7. <u>HEY, A REAL HIGH WALL BILL
   DOWN HERE!</u>
                the theater at Segesta is
                watching clouds of many faces
                pass by

1/1/70
for W.E. Tickell jr.

9. <u>from a letter to Tim Longville</u> (4/12/70)

    No I have no greek theatre in my backyard
    No I have no backyard
                          and shacks like mine
        is all I see
     but it would not bother me a garden with
        (every once in a while) a greek temple
  in some far corner
        (out of sight)

10. PLAYING CHESS WITH ADRIANO
for Adriano Spatola

looks like he wants to eat
my queen. My king says no
by the hair drags her
into the kitchen: this is no way to
get castrated /and/ "From when
my knights disappeared
I move with a certain difficulty
(more slowly)"
               PAY ATTENTION
               ROOK
               TO THE
(PANIC) the queen (PANIC)
she must have run away (she told the
press she didn't like how
everyone was using her without
restraint   WITHOUT A MINIMUM
OF
STRA-
TEGY/ one of the many
       things I lack

: a shower that works
: a mountain outside my door

4/21/70

11. <u>**CONCERNS**</u> : <u>**ROCKS**</u>

Syracuse salmon beyond the door
blue   the white gravel the yellow flowers
the gulf   "at any hour of the day
at any moment you want"

. on a breakneck of rocks
. mon regard tomba sur une pierre.

       what kind of sickness
  pl
     astic preserves us for the future
desolation/ we will be here no longer/ not
many will notice our
long absence
"so much obsessed, said GN, by time"
what can I do if I can make less
<u>HANG-UPS / RELAX / HAND AX</u>

4/17/70

17. THE NEXT DAY TO BE EXACT

surely I prefer hawks above the river
    certain types of mushroom
the mountain I miss
    (outside my door)
must be no less than 1000-1200m.
cedars pines cypresses maples rhododendrons
    (when the light leaves
    we use French gas lanterns
after two day of sirocco at 9 in the morning
I drank the juice of 5 oranges
note that: the temperature has risen
        the sky become cloudy
        the door closes
        with more difficulty

---

the neighbor's sheet metal roof
an iron flag in the wind

4/22/70

18. 100% awake
    torrent of words
    screeches the radio
    turn the dial si-
    lence
            refrigerator completely empty
    800m. over there to the northwest
    the great Nicola slips on black shoes
    (thinking of Wittgenstein?)
    before long that branch
    will enter the window
    glass/ dust/ red

    4/24/70

21. things of great abstraction
    grass and spices
    hook an line
    _____

    reason is quite simple

    5/16/70

for Nelo Risi

24. N.R. "Your condor flies high
    lean and sharp or falls down
    from the sky like a rock."
    that's exactly how
    I thought it should be
      I answer you happy
      when the wind blows
      I expect to see
      the roof of my shack
    fly away

    5/29/70

27. "J"
     the trouble with you is that
          you walk too slow
     the trouble with you is that
          you wake up too early or late
     the trouble with you is that
        you pass in a double curve
     the trouble with you is that
        you feel yourself more than necessary in exile
     the trouble with you is that
        when you are here I miss you

    3/10/70

30. *Early morning*
    plans
    thinking of Su T'ung Po
    half-hour less sleep each morning
    can they measure light years
    or is it just like parking
    from one room to another / the shepherd
    sits down easy on a branch: there was
    another earthquake yesterday the radio says /
    continual register
    high and low tide   slack tide
    wooden pier
    600 feet out into the Pacific
    Avila Beach, California
    rain has washed the eastern slope
    year 1083

    3/10/70

34. poetry
    (look you asked me)
    is a kind
    of philosophy of action
    that is
    telegrammatica

    7/20/70

35. continuing in (p)rose
    it's not easy even this morning
    paper tiger / straw dog
    walls standing spitefully
    bar crowded
    we leave again with the decision made

    5/?/70

<u>6/17/70</u>
37. in the limits of the possible
    that is from no place
    colors that change
    seasons that pass
    me here
    why

40. free to leave — to stay
    (the house is the locust tree
    the lizard jumps from a level branch)
    "Digne ou?" "Dans les Hautes Alpes."
    102 years of age
    Alexandra
    irgendhow in the shade
    270m. above sea level   the numbers
    some shacks   their mystery

    8/15/70

41. Ezra Pound and Chairman Mao
    visit the bench
    alongside my hammock
    (the Ponte di Ferro / acropolis of Selinunte
    the Acque Calde / 15km. as the crow flies)
    we always turn to someone
    analyze our own handwriting (HA HA)
    decidedly temporary
    <u>NO WIND (however) IS THE KING'S WIND</u>
    cf. EP. Ran Ti, canto IV, line 97

    8/7/70

AIRMAIL POSTCARDS

(totally free this morning) (fog on)
(fog cleared) (fog off) (drove through
hills) (no new tires for the day)
(even if you can pay) (totally
loose, this morning which is getting
into late morning) (and hungry
we are both very
hungry) (pale blue south sky) (deep
blue north sky) (very hungry) (so
free so loose) (she holds the car
registration in her teeth) (even the
asphalt the parking lot even the
highway grade a paradise) (so
free so loose so hungry this
late morning) (in your Hornet Wagon
1974) (loose/free/hungry)

15/VI/78

(your face your eyes printed
in front of my eyes) (printed
on mountains sky clouds mirages
salted lakes the prairie the
desert) (only when a golden
eagle chased antelopes your face
vanished) (the antelopes
scattered away) (the eagle flew
away) (your face your eyes
reappeared) (printed
in front of my eyes)

21/VI/78
HIGHWAY 80, WYOMING

(I see poems as sounds
words architecture)
(shelters that take off)
(become catfish, pumas,
lizards, sparrowhawks,
rattlesnakes) (animals
on their own)

15/VI/78

split words, split phrases, split
images) (split songs, reassembled
split again) (double-faced, many-
faced, with so many
arms) (is this what I want,
what I need?)

23/VI/78
Santa Fe

(working for the emperor
Chinese poets were riding
boats) (rivers and horses
carried their heavy thoughts)
(on tight free lance schedule
I ride planes)
(ALBUQUERQUE) (CHICAGO) (BOSTON)
(haunted by
where and when) (I shall
meet you again)

27/VI/78

(in a show window
3 green/blue/lilac
Monet waterlilies
summer dresses)
(thought of you,
dressing, un–
dressing, water–
landscapes)

26/VI/78

(somewhere in
TRIP OUT & FALL BACK
Joanne mentions
your blue sandals) (everytime
I see your name, it
strikes me)

27/VII/78

(well you know we could
live in so many places)
(Rome would, do, Sperlonga
would do, and what about
Taos) (well, San Francisco
and New York are alright don't
you think/though Bolinas/though the
Sierras have/more space)
(did we forget to name
Marseille Venezia Kyoto
did we say anything about
Firenze Paris Amsterdam)
(well, I'm sure we must
have thought of Siracusa
too) (we are always doing
things like that and we
haven't yet considered
Kabul Heart Katmandu)
(well you know we could
live in so many places

28/VI/78

(since NYC is older than Madrid
I sit barechested read Blaise Cendrars
AT THE HEART OF THE WORLD)
(why should I often with anyone
anywhere) (miss everyone every-
thing everywhere) (even the
Maja Desnuda has moved to
New York) (like the Irish yellow
cab driver who reads 500 pages
books a day) (everyone
everything every-
where)

NYC 5/VII/78

A VIEW IN THE KITCHEN

(late Sunday morning
in a green nightgown
she practices Dai Chi)
(just like toothbrushing
she declares)

NYC 9/VII/78

20/IV/78 NEW MEXICO HIGHWAY 25 DREAM
(James Koller told me days ago crossing
Kentucky or Indiana of a hallucination
he had while driving) (a huge bison
hangs head down from the sky, drinks
champagne from a huge crystal cup
standing on the highway painted prairie
green) (I wake up, Jim is driving, the
car is filled in by a squeaky Mexican
woman song, I see a mountain, the
perfect illustration for Ezra Pound's
Chinese Characters As A Medium For Poetry)

(17/V/78 SAN JUAN RIDGE DREAM) (a
Kachina altar: my 2 $ blue face
Kachina doll is glued on that
redwood shake Bill Brown gave me
in Bolinas Nov. 1967) (slightly above
her head, on the left a Pacific island
green snail, on the right a rattler)
(same day, 2 o'clock afternoon I
meet a 3 feet long rattlesnake &
say to Will Staple who nearly stepped
on it, "Rattlesnake Woman is very
kind to her friends" & run back to
the cabin to get Giona so he can see
his first rattlesnake)

MAJAKOVSKJI IN NEW YORK

(want want want)
(what you mean by
want) (want 3 Cadillac
5 Mercedes 7 Chevrolet)
(want want want)
(what do you mean by want)

?/V/78

TARGET

13 poems and inks for Annabel Levitt

mental one

(a few hits of the keys) (finally
for once) (she would like that
it would never end) (to focus)
(the problem is choice)
(finally for once) (a few
hits of the keys)

15/II/78
for J.L. Godard

mental two

―――――――――――

(record snowstorms) (impossible appointments) (Gertrude Stein's fingernails) (or rather) (record snowstorms on impossible appointments) (Gertrude Stein's fingernails)

?/II/78 Napoli
for Ray Johnson

for "ten", dieci, they say "teen"

(hanging out in Amsterdam) (should we
go???) (not even eels will step
on our toes) (how does a pickup
look) (going to Surinam)
(going to Darjeeling) (going to
Georgetown Island, Maine) (is Buddha
spreading???) (blue circles on the
back of one hand) (the tropical
museum is not the topical museum)
(il flauto magico, bicycles and
canoes) (tante cose belle, salad
comes to the table) (mon attention
fut attire par) ("teen")
(a little bell)

7/III/78 Amsterdam
from a collaboration with
Harry Hoogstraten
& Anne Waldman

geographic indian names for Giulia Niccolai
leaving for California

———————————————

COTATI   CUCAMONGA
GUALALA   LOMPOC
MALIBU   MORONGO
NAPA   NATONA
NIPOMO   OJAI
OLEMA   PETALUMA
TAHOE   TAMALPAIS
TOMALES   TOPANGA
YUBA   YALLO BALLY

?/III/78

It's our turn.
I think so.
Filippo il Baleno:
our master.
I think so.
Many bows.
Many boats?
The Vikings were here.
What did they do.
White pines
birch trees
mica sparks.
Eric the Red.
Vinland.

19/III/78

> como el mas triste rey de los mercados
> arde Giordano Bruno eternamente
> > Rafael Alberti

(the philosophers of once: Idea
Spirit & History contained in a
single same form) (now look at
Idea sitting in a skyscraper
directing Spirit by telex who
works in a factory) (History
she is a streetwalker) (what
has changed in the market, los
mercados: Spirit rightly
doesnt want to work for Idea who
pollutes History who is
a streetwalker)

2/VIII/78 Ferrara
for Giovanni d'Agostino
& Gianantonio Pozzi

to come

(to come as to come as
cream) (to come in dream)
(to come in hawthorn)
(to come in darkness) (to
come in blinding sun)
(to come in green dawn
lightning) (to come in
water which flows)
(to come on smooth warm
boulders) (to come together)
(I come you come we come)

17/VIII/78

il monte verità

---

the mountain is
the same, the truth
changed

19/VIII/78

the inside look

Palazzeschi smiled argutamente
Philip Whalen rolled his eyes, hm hm
they never met, now they do
no piano to sit on (target)
an old man dragging 4 suitcases
(target) we dont want to discuss the
situation (target) boring newspaper for
stealing notations (target) one girl
comes in one eye goes out the other
(target) sulle infinite onde della
pelle (target,target) yes, we exist
no, we arent on mescaline
no, we arent on anything
no Allen, I dont know about
generalizations

12/XI/78 NYC

(hey then how are you doing) (…)
(hey then what are you saying) (…)
(listen, you know how I miss you) (…)
(yes, I'm still in New York) (…)
(yes, I went to the dentist again
his name is Victor) (…)
(listen, when are you coming) (…)
(if you decide at the last moment
have you any idea when it will be
this last moment) (…)
(ok, good, then I hug you) (…)

(the extreme indigence of
telephone conversations)

14/XI/78
for E.
& Ted Berrigan

short cut

(the improbable the impossible the unexpected
the sudden) (an operation done with no
haste) (all the possible corners of
the world) (he bows, becomes Monkey, the
wise monkey) (her shoes scattered on
the floor) (even solitude has advantages)
(today the word EVERYTHING recurs)
(one should give it a WHOLE existence)
(ALL OF EVERYTHING, never enough)
(a big bed now very distant)
(a state of grace which comes which goes)
(the same window by day by night)

15/XI/78 NYC
for E.

on the running highways of the mind, mind
you, everything is exceptional:
troubadours palmtrees pyramids the
Pacific along the dunes of a lagoon
Piero della Francesca talks to Jim
Dine — Cy Twombly green bridges yellow
billboards, add all you want
with gesture casual & easy
"donne che avete intelletto d'amore"
an infernal well-devised machine
WHAT DO THESE PEOPLE EAT, WHAT DO THEY
DRINK under the belly if clouds
through Illinois
I read Paul Blackburn, we're in Barcelona
a tree becomes a person, a person becomes
a tree, which kind of tree
7th 6th 5th 4th St. the Bowery
large stretches of fenced-in black
earth — "wanna hear what I wrote," she
says, Cheyenne Wyoming, the through express
coach, 19/XI/78, INTERSTATE 80

THE X BOOK

1.

if somebody very
mistakenly thinks
necessity endurance and price
of his for instance car
superior to those of this for instance
poem, here is an occasion unique
to change his mind

10/24/82

2.

it is advisable to re-read carefully
the previous page
also
it is advisable to read carefully
the next page

10/?/82

3.

to cover totally and thoroughly
with creepers evergreen or not
all the skyscrapers of
NYC SF Seattle Cincinnati Kansas City
to start with

10/19/82

4.

à propos of the peninsula
shaped as a boot
will it reach the knee
or climb all the way
till brushing the groin
of the doubtless long leg
of Miss Europe?
caressing her between
Venice and Trieste?

10/22/82

5.

watching the television off
watching the television on
etc. etc. 10/1/82

6.

x as projection mirror track shadow unknown factor
x as to multiply to block to cancel to sign
x as to balance to cross october ten
x as x hour and even x = little rabbit

4/7/83
for Meret Oppenheim

7.

<u>technicalities</u> to <u>Giovanni Anceschi</u>

there are
among travelers
absent-minded travelers
and there are thoughts
lost while traveling
by absent-minded travelers
but there is no
lost
thought
office

7/4/83

SURPRISE

fast lane
slow motion
full moon
empty space
desert rats
no return
big smile

19/X/86

POINT OF VIEW

I don't know if it
gives the idea
but the point of view
of this point of view
is a point of view
without view

29/X/86

<u>"il faut être
    impossible"</u>

(if I had a spare
toothbrush
   I would sleep here
right now)

22/II/86
VENEZIA
*for Tom
    Raworth*

GIRLS

eating rice
glancing at
lovely Utamaro
faces — also
eating rice

20/IV/86
FUKUOJI-CHO
KYOTO

(I disappear)
(said the monk)
(going home)

6/V/86

for instance dear Jaime de Angulo
your book of 60 and more years ago
which I've translated came out
I imagine you'll be happy about it
the title wasn't changed by me
I didn't choose the cover
I imagine you already know all this
the fact of telling it puts me
in a slightly better mood

★

for instance dear Ted Berrigan
what a laugh you would have if
I would tell all the little
shitty things going on —
you were and are among
the best and in a few minutes
I'll read "from your elegant
period" as you say in a
dedication joking but not too
much — I'll tell you that
the world is becoming far less
elegant every day I imagine
you already know all this
the fact of telling it puts me
in a slightly better mood
a dead poet and one alive
can laugh at it all

★

for instance dear Franco Beltrametti
when you too will have reached the spirits
will there be some poet
some of the best ones
who'll write to tell you
two or three things not bad at all?

just because he has got to tell them
in order to get
in a slightly better mood
    ★

23/V/85

HALF OF IT

Ted Berrigan wrote a list poem called
People who died
Now he died too
There is no way around it
Outside it is raining
I remember Ugetsu Monogatari
About traveling in time and space
The pilot a ghost princess
A japanese movie
Today it is full moon
I just finished glancing thru
Vargas a Swedish magazine
Where Ben Vautier says REGARDEZ AILLEURS
I already said : outside it is raining
But I haven't said : it is past midnight
Now I said it
I can hear my son now seventeen
Breathing in his sleep
A while ago he was improving his reading
On the Italian comic Diabolik
Then he practiced his electric guitar
I wonder what and how are doing so and so
Sure I'd love to love her and I do
I wonder if next year I should keep a journal
I haven't done that for years
84 sounds good for it
8 is the ∞ INFINITE standing
And 4 after all is half of it
Good night Mr. Brian Eno
KING'S LEAD HEAD

22/X/83

UND SO WEITER

let's get it straight from the
beginning ■ this is one of those
things with a given end ■ which
in this case will be same as
title ■ (because remember there is
a title which I won't translate
in order not to ■ offend anyone)
am I playing cat & mouse? ■
no ways, you're no cat nor
mouse and me either ■ I'm
even not the detached observer
■ I'm the person making up
this thing of his own ■
like it or not ■ take it or
leave it ■ of course I could
make up something else
■ it's all about a common
frame of mind ■ look at it
carefully ■ und so weiter

AND SOON IT WAS TILT

(I don't say where) (I don't say
 from whom ■ to steal a line) (a
piece of phrase) (you ■ killed my
 heart) (mind does its best) ■ recal-
ling men) (recalling women) (Neander-
 ■ thal for instance) (I see the
sleeper ■ breathing) (and there are
 lines which ■ nobody wants) ("the
devil impatience sweeps ■ the
 angelic plain somnolence") (she
was ■ simple) (rather well educated)
(magnetic ■ tapes rustle) (eyelids
 kerchiefs) (the ■ metal pinball
 rushed towards the flippers) ■
and soon it was tilt) (there was
 even a good fix ■ for her)
 (fine mushrooms and cookies
 ■ the praised electronic
wonders) (on the ■ wide meadow
 gentian blue) (the atmosphere ■
 generated by volcanoes and the
 oceans too) ■ (healed) (she
opens her eyes and) (untranslatable)
 ■ (unspeakable) (she wakes up
and) (mind does its best)

23/VII/83 (Milano)

PROFONDO PENSIERO BILINGUE ★ DEEP BILINGUAL THOUGHT

above all we can think
soprattutto possiamo pensare
at least we think so
almeno cosi pensiamo

11/VIII/82

the movie I would like to
see tonight ♦ starts with a
big scene of horses ♦ galloping
into the dusty main street ♦
suddenly torn from deep
afternoon sleep ♦ each horse
has a rider of course ♦ but
what really matters is horses
♦ from there the movie takes
off ♦ without any loss of
speed ♦ till the unexpected
slow end ♦ which has a
still life intensity ♦ though
it all happens in the open
♦ under a huge sign
hanging on the horizon ♦
which reads:
WELCOME & GOODBYE

because I am here and because
    you came back from Mindanao
which is a long way away even
flying, and because you stayed
    one night and took a shower
        I am writing this, Mindanao
    has a very specific sound I
    never realized before, an island
    three times larger than Kyushu
which has a very different sound
    but what I wanted to say is how
        you and islands and me and sounds
        do sometimes get together like
on this page with many ands

14/I/81

      don't refuse the muse who
        wakes you up
to transmit your self portrait
   with one finger only
which doesn't look at all
like the one of van Gogh
   with his one ear only
but rather to a polaroid
more black than white
shot with one finger only
 like this self portrait
  under dictation of the muse
    typed with one finger only

21/III/81

MESSAGE

I am in front
where there's light
high up to the left
or down low to the right
if you call me
it could be
that I can't hear you
rise your voice
even in the dark you
will notice the lilac
pawlonia blooming over
the ping pong table
and if I am not here
I will be back soon
after midnight
you know where
the key is —
and on the table you
find "The Cult of Tara"
and on the fridge
the tea you like

10/V/81

Tom Raworth & Franco Beltrametti
Val Maggia / 1990

THREE FOR NADO

COUACS

*for Demetrio Stratos
and Bernard Heidsieck*

SBALLO
SBERLA
STECCA

STACCO
SCATTO
SGARRO

SCIPPO
SMACCO
SCACCO

MATTO

31.V.89 MILANO-NYC

**AIRPLANE
SONG**
for Valeria Magli

you're silly
therefore you're out
because you're
happy to fly

31.V.89

CRUCIAL MATTERS
to Robert Creeley

come here
see it in print
keep it together
give me a break
and never be done
with all of it

hummingbird
on snapdragon

?.VI.89

Franco Beltrametti & house
Elakawee, Nevada City, California / 1974

CALIFORNIA TOTEM

dedicated to P.W.

on lilac purple HACIENDA DE VALDEZ bus
the Moving Theatre drives to San Francisco
Tantra Circus Solstice Celebration
★

ladies with colds smoke homegrown
their lovely Deva faces smile
over their skulls
★

in the back: masks costumes drums kids
★

at Stinson Beach gas station
James Koller's Thomas the Siberian wolf
barks out of my memory
while pine trees tops shine
and Lew Welch's turkey buzzards wheel
over roaming cows
★

"hey, we forgot the container to put out the fire
after the jump through the ring of flames"
★

BIG TOTEM ANIMALS MASKS UNDER DIM GREEN LIGHT
★

out of the city, into the dark
★

the first land signs I saw 1967
                coming in by cargo from Japan
were car lights
on this road along the coast

21/12/74
for Piero Resta

Dear Jack Spicer

   I watch with curiosity and surprise faces bodies
words
as you know I write from outside San Francisco
   and other objects surface from the past, float towards
some 4 hours drive east
   a crowded place called future, while sitting
I don't know how patient you are
   on a bamboo chair in a basement
but I know you are dead
   the starry Berkeley winter evening is the present
Groucho Marx said he would never enter a club
   plans & tickets always need adjustments
that would accept him as a member
   "the ghosts the poems were written for"
so it is January and I am alone
   "cannot hear the noise they have been making"
I greet your small vocabulary
   regarding past present and future
that lamp that horse that continent

1-7/1/75

SOME ARCHITECTURAL NOTES
for Lawrence Ferlinghetti

... (there are many strange objects drifting
in the world) ...
... (bricolage, bricoleur) ...
... (mental smog equals
no space) ...
... (we look through the windows, come in & out
through the doors) ...
... (a blue sky winter morning
the master plan for the urban scene
— an earthquake? — a tidal wave?) ...
... (a wasp city hanging from a branch) ...
... (rules codes money) ...
... (beaten earth & trails versus
highways) ...
... (space begins with our eyes & ears
skin nose tongue & mind) ...
... (as a rule everything made up can be
changed substituted adjusted
demolished reinvented) ...
... (if you get free from the hook
of dominant language, language-dope) ...
... (then, who decides for whom
& how) ...
... (a space
so transparent
you don't need
to be aware of) ...

13/1/7

Dreamed smooth plans: everyone and everything was
Taken care of. The first sun rays play leaves shade theatre
On the wet window. And I forgot the plans.
Bolinas Mesa a green boat: coyote brush parsley hemlock and rocks
Woven together. Mud roads puddles mirrors. Sky and water
Till China and Japan. All the way down to Chile.
All the way up to Alaska.

17/12/74

<u>Sesshu</u>: an exploding rock
<u>Soami</u>: the sound of a temple bell in the evening
<u>Hakuin</u>: skully & eyeballs
<u>Max Ernst</u>: petrified cities, birds & moons
<u>Tanguy</u>: I recall ice
<u>Sam Francis</u>: floating blue green yellow orange red whirlwind
<u>Piero della Francesca</u>: oval head, bodies-columns
<u>Le Douanier Rousseau</u>: a jungle scene, with a black panther

20/12/74

Dante's vision is real
he saw it   (didn't want to miss it)
        (got his share of angels)
Villon, Francois — wisdom of the gutters???
Artaud-le-Momo
not on sale.
        (remarques, wrote Gertrude Stein to
have said to Hemingway, remarques are not
literature)

?/12/74

Like forty thousand years ago
Spirit Animals
Feathers & Furs
Claws & Paws
Iron Dolls & Metal Masks
X-rays bodies In & Out
Neither Living nor Dead
Painted Drums & Floating Coats

14/12/74

I feel the warmth of my ears close to my head.
I am sitting by an aluminum window.
I am taking up space.
The dark green wooden trunk to my right
Is occupying space too,
In front of the couch covered with blankets
On which I sit.
The aluminum window is to my right, the sky is luminous
White fog behind & around geraniums, a driftwood greenhouse
& a cypress tree.
The stove to my left is very small & warm & has four funny
Insect's legs, an iron cubic beetle, the name CORONA is
Cast on its lowest door.
The stove's legs shine.
Everything with a body has a volume & is doing this space
Which otherwise wouldn't be there.

10/12/74

If dawns have fingers
Fingers have drums
Drums have dreams
And dreams have almost
Everything. If everything has
Dawns
Fingers
Drums
Dreams, than
What's the news? The news are
Very old,
Call the owls.
They may tell you.

7/12/74

Bolinas Ridge, douglas fir, puffballs
Amanita Muscaria, Moon Islands
Mouse teeth in fox shit
All shapes of clouds
The iron sea the lilac sea the sea sea
Mushroom skin scratched changes colour
With clouds light changes speed

23/11/74
with Peter Warshall

California: from caliente (hot) fuerno (oven), at least
I thought so. Now I read in a corner of Shelter Book how
California was the virtuous heroine of a popular trash
dime chivalry romance read by everybody in Spain, from
Ignacio da Loyola to the oversea soldiers. From which the
actual California, through conquests and missions. Dizzy
Lady California, Hot Oven Lady, got married with Condor.
Lao Tzu and Kuksu were there too. Coyote, uninvited, came
with his tail. He didn't have a chance to read California
till later, there were no public libraries nor bookstores.

25/10/74

Where you think to be — in Mongolia?
Stretching your legs from Mount Tamalpais
All the way to Amazonia, El Dorado, Manoa?
Holding on your palms the minarets of
Persia Turkey and North Africa.
Standing on top of Mount Fuji Mount Etna.
Floating along the Black Current.
How many stars have you eaten, how many times
You made it out of hell?
Who you think to be, Marcel Duchamp
Su Tung Po Paolo Uccello? What kind of bird
Are you, nesting on what kind of tree?
If imagination doesn't provide no survival
Income, why don't you get a job, in Mongolia
Or Amazonia Persia North Africa.
Why don't you answer, why don't you.
Playing mirror, playing the mirror's game
Is that what you are up to?
English is not your native language
Language is not your native speech.
Where have you stashed all those minarets.
Your hands are as empty as a stretch
Of salted desert. Applepie Queen has
Opened her stands along the silkway, her hands
Taste like honey. You still have not told me
Who the fuck you are. I don't want to know it
Anymore. Turquoise. Yellow amber.
Seaweed. Hear the drums, the voices.
You will meet them. You will be ready.

7/12/74

PETER IN THE WOLF

The play occurs in a cave on the banks of the Upper Kanavah River. Outside the time is nowadays Charleston/Virginia. Chemical plants (Monsanto) and animal rendering plant skyscrapers (Mac Adam's Animal Eatings) vie for the light. Inside the cave the light shifts from dim to reddish-black to extremely flashy any second now. The people in the cave are dancing. They are. No, the play happens in Marsala, Sicily. The scene is covered — you can't actually see through — the scene is covered with all kinds of city dump. Where are all the town dump men-in-charge gone? They are dancing, strike is on, all out. More dump, you see? The railway to Trapani is lonely on that stretch of the sea. Marsala Florio gloomy factory wall dominates the landscape. It is so very sad & beautiful & dry & there is no traffic, no trains, no cars, only them, dancing on top of the dump, like many Shivas. No, the play really happens in Bolinas/California at Susanna Acevedo's house. A chicklet is laying on the floor. No, this play really happens at Larry Kearney's house a little way south of Susanna Acevedo's house. "My father died yesterday and I'm holding an old-fashioned Irish wake," Larry says, and slumps to the floor. A monstrous image of Peter Rabbit appears in the mouth of the cave with blood on his mouth. Each person in the audience is handed a bone. Right on. & the play is happening at Smiley's & Jim Gustafson is the bartender & two guys drive in the bar on their 125 ccm bike & the blonde lady who runs the place tells them: I'm going to phone your mother & your father as well. It is 2 a.m. — no way out. I'm going to call all your ancestors. It's a long trip, but they will come.

17/11/74

The eleventh day or was it the seventh
How strange how remarkable
I'm nailing since weeks and haven't hit
More than 3 times
The same finger in the same place
I deserve the whole Dutch Girl Icecream Float
Disparate nuts of disparate colour and taste

In 1849 there were at least 14 main settlements
Within 2 miles of nowadays downtown Nevada City

There were Maidu people and got wiped out while for instance
Since 1851 Empire Mine scored 2000 millions $ gold

The miners were very happy to die of silicosis
They all were very grateful especially the Chinese
They all loved to die for Empire Mine

A very telegrammatic real fast poem by N.Y. poet
Anne Waldman goes

<u>Hurricane</u> / <u>insane</u> / <u>je t'aime</u>

Time to quit real fast

Galaxies are stolen diamonds

Nanao said

?/11/74

It was a pumpkin, a she-pumpkin, running
Right?
No, it was a melon, a watermelon, a she-watermelon
Running & rolling downhill.
No, it wasn't a watermelon.
Her body was covered with fur.
No, her body wasn't covered with fur.
She had no tail, she had no head.
It was a car, a 4 wheel drive car
A car with a tongue
A car with a pink tongue
A car with a fur tongue
Singing fur word songs
To you.
No, it wasn't a car, it was rain, fur rain
The roof was leaking
It was Monday in the evening
The week wasn't started
Dust season was over.

27/10/74

WALTER BENJAMIN

Walter Benjamin's ideal was
To write a book of quotes
— book tracks out & in
               I am my only visitor
& this is
the quote

21/10/74

                WHAT'S YOUR NAME
                WHAT'S YOUR GAME
                WHAT'S YOUR TOTEM
                WHAT'S YOUR RITE
                          & WHAT'S YOUR TUNE (HOW LONG AGO
WAS IT TOLD
          ROCKS FLOAT
          MIND CLOUDS
          THE MAIDU
          THE SIOUX
                    DRIFTING VULTURES WASPS & RATTLERS
ALL THE MARX BROTHERS
JEAN LUC GODARD & ALL THE STARS
THE WHOLE PEKING OPERA ZAP & BANG & ZAP
BANG BANG (CONDOR DANCE TAKES OVER L.A., PALERMO
& EL PASO

21/10/74

> *"Siamese cats are very*
> *demanding. Unlike*
> *turtle shells."*
>
> *for Peter Warshall*

NOW PRIMITIVE MEANS

* ★ sealing off skylights
  silicone glue all over the fingers

* ★ second hand truck
  roaches compost messy greenhouses

* ★ streetpeople (dogeaters) playing football
  don't count goals

* ★ traffic jammed downtown hell's angels

* ★ sometimes it is easy survival
  sometimes it s hard & harsh
  cool soft dark fur
  imagination bodies
  totem heart beats

* ★ it's all real it's all real yes it is

* ★ you are part of it
  Garcia Lorca duende
  Sioux-Zen total ease

* ★ wings wings wings

9/10/74

DHARMA POETRY READING REPORT

On my birthday they were eight to walk on stage in a row. Philip Whalen was leading with a strange elephant stroll, he was the master of ceremonies. They sat on green velvet chairs & on red & yellow meditation pillows, behind the microphones. They started reading one after the next strictly keeping time, 15 minutes each. Michael McClure read about Peru & lamas & blue sky lakes. Anne Waldman got introduced as a celebrated poet from N.Y., she read a long I'm an automobile woman, I'm a fast talking woman, I'm a woman who can operate the machinery, I'm a velvet woman etc I'm a woman woman poem & she was like Janis Joplin dynamite back on stage keeping the beat with boots stomping the floor. Joanne Kyger ended the reading. Philip introduced her as a long neglected poet, Joanne couldn't see what she wanted to read so lights & table got rearranged, she made no mistakes & finished with a thank you that's me — & the reading was over. The champagne served in the basement was expensive & the San Francisco night was very wet.

7/10/74

sudden dawn wind
        each pine
a different sound
            (dreams & nightmares, do the kitchen & get running water on the Noh platform)

13/9/74

THE LAUNCHING OF THE SKUA

        The day of the launching of the boat in the lagoon a
small crowd had gathered to see it happen, truck & crane
& trailer & boat. The crane had rehearsed in the morning.
A man with a yellow safety hard hat came & said sorry the
trailer didn't make it, it will come tomorrow. Never mind
said Peter everybody here looks like unemployed & can come
back tomorrow. The boat was ready to leave the hill slope
where it was built the last ten years or so, it looked
smaller than it used to & had flowers on the keel. I thought
of Jack Boyce, the boat would have to stay one more night
on the hill. I wondered what Jack would have to say about
that. The breeze was whistling through the dry grass. Three
turkey vultures came circling above us like flying TV. It
doesn't mean anything since there are only three, a lady
said. One of the birds did a blink fast flap with its tail,
a sort of greeting. Everybody left & only Joanne & Peter &
me stayed a while longer, sitting on the slope. Boat launching
aficionados always come 24 hours ahead.

8/10/74
for Ebbe Borregaard

I think of my mountain cabin & it is very remote
I wish a girl with clear bright eyes full of grace
Would appear down the trail moving like a panther
With all her wisdom & give me a hug

?/10/74

"Before vanishing into vague
Somebody else's memories
Of Pleistocene or the late seventies
I wish to state my presence
My having been here" with

NO MIRROR TO KEEP CLEAN

The breeze the sun
The fog bank white on blue
Compostpiles going to winter garden

TRANSPARENT

   "durchsichtig"

HASTA LUEGO

No Granada Siracusa Rio de la Plata
No Bagdad Arizona

Noontime Bolinas Paradise Valley
See you later
Home Movie

31/8/74
for Bill Brown

UPSTREAM MAIDU KALI YUBA YUGA FLOW
for Allen Ginsberg

On New York Blues you
Wrote to Franco who
Is building in another country
On Green Yuba River I
Write for Allen who
Saw it flow
Upstream

9/7/74

At falling shack meadow
A crushed dying lizard
I finish with my right boot heel
Why wheels death
A few steps to find lizard number two
Its head one eye
An open paw a hand a left foot

GREETING   LIZARD

Leather totem ghost sign
In truck tracks
In red dust

24/8/74

Ururulumunuzu at China Flats
Ururulumunuzu bats wings flap
Ururulumunuzu two porcupine came
Ururulumunuzu didn't stay too long
Ururulumunuzu coyotes howling weirdly
Ururulumunuzu all night I thought of you
Ururulumunuzu ururulumu ururu uru u

20/7/74

(...she says: dig it. Be my mirror. The mirror to
my time. Humbly & gratefully. White buckeye flowers cones
are gone. Welcome. Look at the white frog in the sink. Look
at the axe blade on the tin roof. There goes your portrait
painted for you. Green blue waves & lines. See how they
meet. You will cry. The portrait says: why not, in the same
sleeping bag. It's my portrait, she says, can't you read.
Iron birds fly as in Padmasambhava's prophecy. Can you hear
me through the Bay dark air ...)

?/7/74

The myth of history — Independence Day isn't
Annexation Day — Which is another day later on
At Tyler Foothill Road mailbox turnoff
Independence Day tourists cars zoom by
Cherokee Diggins blinding moonscape
A B-52 cuts the blue sky in two
Wait for a ride — bring longbolts home

4/7/74

FIRE ACCESS ROAD PEOPLE QUOTES

"unhinge the door type of poetry like you get the door out burn it & sell the hinges at Len's, next trip to town"

"with a ridgepole like that there will always be a lady under your roof"

"Get some more Mahayana shit on that stump"

"4 x 8 can span a whole life"

?/6/74

(ABOUT YOU & ME)   (AN INTERVIEW)

me: if the most important thing is
        boots — what's next
no,   she says, boots are only among the
        important things, they are not
        the most important thing
me: OK, then what is another
        very important thing

the place, she says, the place
        where you put your body & in good places
        I take off my boots

& she did — (thinking of a little town
out of Paris) "J'ai vachement envie d'apprendre
tu peux pas t'imaginer.

21/6/74

"Don Bartolomeo
never scolded, he never said
anything,
he only looked"
                      Jaime de Angulo

      GET 12-FOOTERS 4 X 8 AT SAGE'S
           GET THE OUT OF BED
   GET 4 X 6 AT THE WOBBLY GHOST FLUME
              GET LAGBOLTS
               IRONWASHERS
               DIG 9 HOLES
          GET WHITE GRAVEL
           AT SHADY CREEK
              GET REBARS
           GET PEYOTE TAR
            GET THE MAIL
          GET A DRAWKNIFE
          A CHISEL A DRUM
             GET A DRUM
     GET A DRUM AT CHINA FLATS
& SHE WAS BLUE & SHE WAS GREEN & HER HAIR
        WAS RED HENNA HAIR
THE ROCKS DOWN THE RIVER WERE SMOOTH
& SHE WAS BLUE & SHE WAS GREEN & HER HAIR

?/6/74

Franco Beltrametti at Galeria Attila, Bellinzona / 1994

PAINTINGS

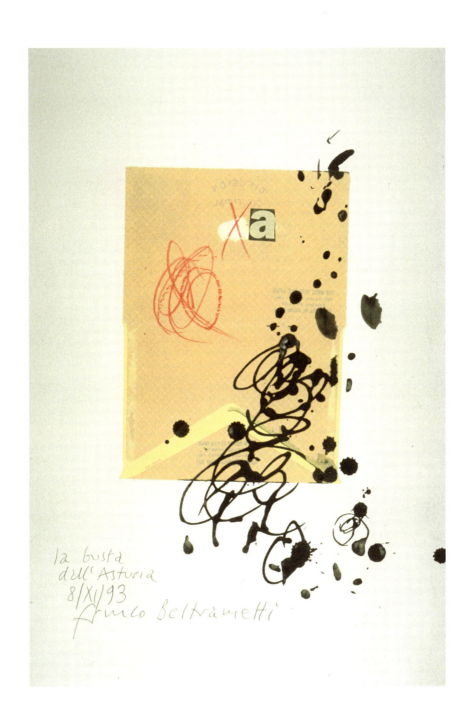

la busta
dell'Asturia
8/XI/93
Franco Beltrametti

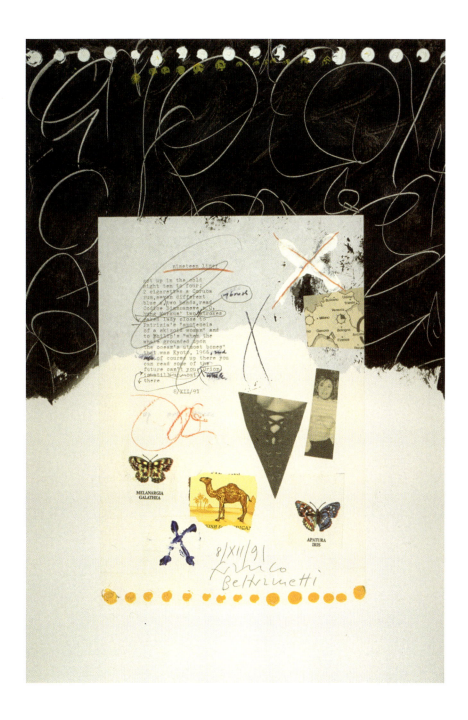

THE WAY TO
WITTGENSTEIN'S
GRAVE

Franco
Beltrametti
18/VIII/94

BROADSIDES
&
CONCERTINA BOOKS

(published by Ascona Presse, Ascona, Switzerland, 1991)

MONTE GENROSO

monte generoso
4500 feet above the lake
its cliff buddha faces
its trees dakini hair
in sky blue lights the way
to the white clouds
repeat towers on rocky heads
nothing but emptiness
is what they say

3/III/90

(published by Longhouse, Green River, Vermont, 1995)

POTTERY   POETRY   &   HORSES
Anto Verbatim

I was working with Kathy Sanchez in San Ildefonso Pueblo.
It was early but it wasn't late for a coffee at O'Casados,
a restaurant of Espanola, N.M. One couldn't smoke but in a
dark room with a large TV on and a door open on the kitchen.
A man came in and said, I am here because I smoke. Me too,
I said. I am Roberto Garcia, he said, I am famous, I am a cowboy,
what you like. Pottery and poetry, I told him. Poetry? he
said, I like horses.

13/X/94
from MUGENA JOURNAL

(published by Longhouse, Green River, Vermont 2004
with an introduction by James Koller)

I TEND TO SIMPLIFY EVERYTHING

Franco Beltrametti created his life much as he wrote or painted, from what seemed to many others unrelated "found" bits & pieces. Blaise Cendrars, another Swiss, provided Franco an early life model. Franco's trip to Japan paralleled Cendrars' trans-Siberian rail trip. Franco noted Cendrars' many sea trip to the Americas, the car trip to California & his travel writings, especially his "postcards", which suggested a form Franco later embellished upon. Franco arrived in the US for the first time in 1967 on a Japanese freighter with his American wife Judy & young son Giona. He felt he needed to discover in America what until then was denied to him as a result of his father's family giving up their Mendocino homestead, returning to Switzerland soon after the 1906 San Francisco earthquake. For Franco late 60s California seemed a frontier, a place of possibility, "A place," he once said, "where you can easily disappear." Jaime de Angulo, like Franco, a European, arrived in California as a young man soon after Franco's family had left the state. He too became part of the life Franco built. Once he had discovered de Angulo's Indians In Overalls, the book inspired Franco's back country life & his poems. Back in Europe, Franco went on to translate the novel, Don Bartolomeo into Italian, returning de Angulo too to Europe.

James Koller 2 August 2003

LUXEMBOURG POSTCARD

?white clouds through blue
sky or blue clouds through
white sky?

21/V/87

WAGON 136

I eat two bananas
four Belgian ladies
stare at me
severely

27/V/87

much
sky
many
tree clouds
many
cloud clouds
much lagoon much
water
much
alone
alone how much
enough

9/IX/87 *Burano*

ZEITSCHRIFT FUER ALLES N. 10
today's version of it

(what is this noise?
(let's call it music
(sometimes I say to myself
   do I have a name for that thing?
(have I seen that movie? and where
   and when and what was it called?
(the beginning was the end
(<<when I answered the phone
   I knew right away that she had
   the wrong number>>
(<<god lives in a fridge
   handing out words of wisdom>>
(beware of German philosophy
   I say to those girls that take over
   my dream in Oklahoma

25/IX/87
for Dieter Roth

PHONE CALL TO REIDAR EKNER

"We are on E4 250 km south of
Stockholm what should we do?"
ANSWER: "Drive carefully."

27/XI/87

isn't it the
same thing everywhere that
it isn't at all the same
thing everywhere?

16/XII/87

THALIA VERBATIM

I tend to simplify everything: if
he likes to pour his
tea in the pinball machine
why worry?

25/XII/87

some
poems
have
a
title
some
don't

6/VII/88

MISCELLANEOUS POEMS

from books, magazines and anthologies

{*books*}

from: Trattamento Micologico Del Mondo
Caos Press, Melano, Switzerland 1978 with Marcello Angioni

MICOLOGICAL TREATMENT OF WILLIAM BURROUGHS

Let me start at the beginning.
Those who don't know the story
I can feel the closing in,
feel them out there making
repugnant fungal growths,
manifestations of parasitism and decay
phosphorescent writing in blue metal
that filled the room
once looked at the mushroom with
a discriminating eye.
Indeed in his brain like
Chinese flowers — Myriads of floating
sex prearrangements.
I could talk to you for
a long time about the words

from: 19 PERMUTAZIONI
Edizione Inedite & Scorribanda Productions,
Venezia, Italy/Riva S. V., Switzerland, 1986

(everything) (nothing) (a little)
(everything) (a little) (nothing)
(nothing) (everything) (a little)
(nothing) (a little) (everything)
(a little) (everything) (nothing)
(a little) (nothing) (everything)

18/II/84

(past) (present) (future)
(past) (future) (present)
(present) (past) (future)
(present) (future) (past)
(future) (past) (present)
(future) (present) (past)

28/2/84

(left) (right) (straight)
(left) (straight) (right)
(right) (straight) (left)
(right) (left) (straight)
(straight) (left) (right)
(straight) (right) (left)

11/XII/85
for Tom Raworth

from: TUTTO QUESTO
Supernova, Venezia, Italy, 1990

no
yes yes
no no no
yes yes yes yes
no no no no no
yes yes yes yes yes yes
yes no yes no yes no yes
no yes no yes no yes no
no no no no no no
yes yes yes yes yes
no no no no
yes yes yes
no no
yes

?/12/80

— lip rouge, european
— wooden comb, japanese
— sewing machine, inlayed likewise
with wood, from Surinam
— profile of a lady by Ghirlandaio,
the colors so fresh
as if painted just today
— each one of us a very particular
case
— something beside the point
something like Kansas City
— seventh, colored pencils

18/2/82
for Bill Berkson

       not my cup of tea
this is not my cup of tea
this   not my cup of tea
this   not my cup of tea
this is not my cup of tea
      not my cup of tea
      not my cup of tea

15/7/82

maybe so maybe not
maybe today maybe tomorrow
maybe now maybe never
maybe here maybe there
maybe high maybe low
maybe short maybe long
maybe warm maybe cold
maybe rich maybe poor
maybe love maybe hate
maybe solid maybe liquid
maybe strong maybe weak
maybe so maybe not

21/9/82

KYOTO SURPRISE

I thought she was
Lady Murasaki
and she was
Lady Murasaki
same face
same soul
1000 years later

?/V/86
for Duncan McNaughton

INFOLIO READER
TODAY'S VERSION OF IT
for Tom Raworth

(lucky man
(outside the kitchen window
  on the fire escape
(any politician will eat
  radioactive food
(the sun goes down
(bombs tend to go off
(you have no imagination
(goodbye to the Bay of Naples
(another tattoo
(the last message comes first
(days pass
(human error
(your cute life
(the early bus
  forever to be lost
(there is no trick
(out there in the country
(hard currency preferred
(this is not the way
(begin again

17/XI/86

qualche	some
parola	word
trovata	found
spostata	displaced
riciclata	recycled
diventata	become
incantata	enchanted

25/II/88

from: TRATATTO NANETTO
Supernova, Venezia, Italy, 1992

THE SALT LAKE CITY DWARF POETS HEADQUARTERS
for Richard Brautigan

Of all places, what an unlikely one to meet for two wandering dwarf poets, Salt Lake City.

Spread on hills with a net of boulevards lined with stern buildings meant to last forever with wide views on endless blinding salted whiteness.

They spot one another on the abandoned sidewalk down in the flats. Crowds of weeds shoot up from the cement cracks.

To rent, sell or lease, reads the weathered sign on the sad gate of a run down warehouse, blocks away from the railway station.

They stare at the sign, read it over and over, stare firmly in one another's eyes, catch deep in there the very same thought.

LONELY NIGHTS

The next thought was fast and drastic: let's move on. Which they did, nodding slightly, going on their separate destinies.

But the intensity of the unspoken vision still lingers in a hidden corner of the memory and sometimes, when absent minded, floats up making them wonder what could it all have been about.

Just spell it once more: THE DWARF POETS SOCIETY HEADQUARTERS, Salt Lake City, Utah 84100.

Dwarf poetry fax piling up on translucent fiberglass tables.

A few lyrical Mormon secretaries Zipping around the remodeled red brick warehouse.

Type this poem, young lady. Fax it to Avignon, France.

A Bitter Campari, Sweety.

Where the fuck is the hash stash?

Thank you, Honey.

Lost thoughts, once caught in one another's eyes floating up in lonely cold winter nights

from: LOGICHE & ILLOGICHE
Giona Editions, Riva S.V., Switzerland, 1994

a distant city
<u>   </u>
        last adios to
<u>   </u>
                Kubla Khan
<u>   </u>
                        flexibly yours

to Joanne Kyger
21/I/94

WET PAINT MOTHERFUCKERS
for a plank

WET PAINT MOTHERFUCKERS
WET MOTHERFUCKERS PAINT
PAINT MOTHERFUCKERS WET
PAINT WET MOTHERFUCKERS
MOTHERFUCKERS WET PAINT
MOTHERFUCKERS PAINT WET

31/III/94

SPIDERMONKEYBABYAND
to Javier Ruiz

(spidermonkeyandbaby)
(spidermonkeybabyand)
(spiderandbabymonkey)
(spiderandmonkeybaby)
(spiderbabymonkeyand)
(spiderbabyandmonkey)

(monkeyandbabyspider)
(monkeyandspiderbaby)
(monkeybabyspiderand)
(monkeybabyandspider)
(monkeyspiderandbaby)
(monkeyspiderbabyand)

(andbabyspidermonkey)
(andbabymonkeyspider)
(andspidermonkeybaby)
(andspiderbabymonkey)
(andmonkeybabyspider)
(andmonkeyspiderbaby)

(babyspidermonkeyand)
(babyspiderandmonkey)
(babymonkeyandspider)
(babymonkeyspiderand)
(babyandspidermonkey)
(babyandmonkeyspider)

Berlin 24/I/94

dear Alan Jones) (after last night via
Pontaccio last beer Frank Sinatra paints
ants) (who wouldn't) (not his aunt Re
gina Margherita who beats connections
out of frozen tricolore Chicago pizzas) (a
Quartet, etc., considering Fer
dinand Leger tenore pre-animist
scream) (ma) (Olson, long life to pre-Roman
oysters & please do take a bow to Cid
Corman in Utano Kyoto) (GIVE US BACK HUGO
BALL) (ARRIDATECE MARCEL DUCHAMP) (study
deeply what is Baruchello all about) (don't
forget Philip Whalen) (On Bear's Head) (see you in
Paris for sushi & sake) (North Dakota ci
aspetta) (ti rendi conto per noi) (dunque
tutti e due amiamo Tsutaka Waichi Sensei che
a Trieste lesse tutto James Joyce) (guarda che 'co
incidenze' combina a Berlino Rolf Langebartels
) (feed-back) (feed-back) (feed-back
) (feed-back)   (verso casa corre il treno sotto la
luna piena   Milano, Eze-sur-Mer, Marseille,
Arles, Paris, Berlin, Mannheim, Basel, Capolago
ⓒ ☏ ♦♣♥♠♣♠♠♥♥♣♣♣♦♦♦☏ xxxxxxxxxxxx

11-27/IV/94

from: TOUT ÇA,
Aiou, Saint-Etienne-Vallée, France 1994

Imagine a japanese american beauty
only her a rose in lots of space
raven black hair and lots of grace

8/II/90

{*magazines & anthologies*}

from: Kuksu, Journal of Backcountry Writing #4 "Work"
edited by Dale Pendell, Nevada City, California 1975

6 DAYS OF WORK FROM A LOST NOTEBOOK

THE RIDGE POETS WORKERS GET UP AT DAWN
HAVE BREAKFAST OUTDOORS
QUOTE KABIR, LADY MURASAKI
MYRDAL CHINESE VILLAGE REPORT N.2
DO LATIN NAMES SUIT OUR LANGUAGE
LIKE AMANITA MUSCARIA ISNT CESAREA
NOW LOOK
THE BRIDGE IS FALLING GOT FUCKED UP
BY A HEAVY LOADED LUMBER TRUCK

★

YOU BETTER LEAVE THEM ALONE
HAVE HIGH NOON DREAMS, THE STARS
   ARE ALL
     YOURS

THE WORLD RENEWAL DIDNT HAPPEN THAT DAY
ANYWAY NOT ALL OF IT

COYOTE WAS THERE : STARING
GREEN TARA WAS THERE, RIGHT??
ON A STUMP
IN THE STONE RING SHE
WAS THERE & HE

HE WAS OUT
THAT'S OF COURSE SOMETHING ELSE
& THE WORLD GOT WHAT IS NEW.
THE BRIDGE KEPT FALLING & EVENTUALLY
REPAIRED & THE LADY HAD THE FLASHLIGHT
IN THE SKY

THE SKY WAS HER POCKET
SHE HAD HOLES IN HER POCKET
LIKE A RIMBAUD
SHE WAS GREEN & BLUE W/HENNA HAIR
THERE WERE POLES TO SKIN

& HER BODY WAS SO YOUNG & TENDER & SOFT

15/5/74

& she was coming & had
henna hair & by now I guess
you got it
the point is what happened
next

20/6/74

AND HER BODY WAS SO YOUNG SO TENDER & SOFT
with all yr 18 years in bloom in my arms
I can take what you can give
& give what you can take
in the curly locks of coming
out of sleep
  (you have a mark above yr left
breast, sd forget it)
  (my tongue taste it call it)
  (my tongue call her Vulture Peak
lady or Blue Monkey Girl)
  (so young & tender & soft)
(I can keep seeing yr. long legs coming out of yellow
pine bark, while I skin poles w/a drawknife)

so maybe we didnt see those
scary cold red & white flashing lights
so you are you & me is me

?/6/74

PS: there is no way to write work poems, there are songs
people sing working together on building strawroofs or
working in the fields — or running wildly on the streets &
she runned & she runned & she runned & her hair was red
& she was the wind of the east

(…sick today, cant work, lie in movable digger pines
shades on the north side of a birdbone frame an old maga-
zine says Garcia Lorca says metaphors are poems' engine,
a humming bird dashes out comes visit perching on a dry
blue oak branch…)

(…later, same day, lilac dusk sky, moon close to full,
cold & pale, bats diving wings flapping zig zag up & down

after mosquitoes, swollen lymph glands pain rising, a weak body, mind hopelessly tied in, floating dream of health & happiness suspended...)

2/7/74

from: AN ALLEGHANEY STAR ROUTE ANTHOLOGY
edited by Franco Beltrametti, Grosseteste, England, 1975

SHE

hey, look at her, *mira, regarde, guarda*
she's *muy guapa*: she
eats cherries, isnt she
today's poem

18/6/74
for H.

NO CAR

me too (as you) dont want
to repeat the same old mistakes
want to be an open meadow
a river bed
fly as a red tail hawk

    (this at dawn
blue monkey lady sleeping at
my side, very
                unusual July rain beating
asphalt paper roof)

want to let you know
want to be a rattlesnake
a rock a wasp no car

9/7/74
for Joanne Kyger

FROM "CONDOR NOTES"

A dying relic of the Pleistocene

You can see the sky
thru the perforate nasal section

"A hunter says 150 condors near an
antelope he had killed
in the latter part of the 19th century"

California big tree
California big condor

"On several occasions Karl
Kuford has seen a California condor
scratch its head with its food
without a waver in the vertical
& horizontal lines of flight"

later in the morning
it's all over
& je t'aime

4/8/74

from: SPERLONGA MANHATTAN EXPRESS
Scorribanda Productions, Riva S.V., Switzerland, 1980

CALL ME QUEEQUEG

I would like to write a sizable book about
tattoos, out of my tattoo eye which is
Queequeg's eye & space would come large & no
borders technology would bother the (heroes
well they are just) people on the side of
vipers bears & pumas, now, pumas are back,
great, ok, but atom war is knocking any
second to Gaeta red light door to (you name
it) say Sakurajima Bay say goodbye May days
the floating word on Tokaido highway
the everyday: tales on tales on tales till
geological starlitted Samadhi, no use is
the use of poetry, remember? I would call
the book: really, I would call it,
call me Queequeg

7/XII/79

from: GROSSETESTE REVIEW, VOL. 13,
edited by Tim Longville, Derbyshire, England, 1980/1981

now the fan is running
now we shall go out
everything remains a mystery
TV broadcasting started 1936 so what
so I'm younger than TV broadcasting
so let's go out, slanted eyes tattoo faces
the Juan de Fuca Strait
imagine islands instead of lines
each letter a tree, water still and wide
no horizon line

27/VI/80
NYC

the first thing I see
opening the eyes (what do they
see) the window and three layers of
white clouds on perfect blue
sky, I'm going to paint them
thinking of Tom Raworth's
typewriter, it's going to
take the whole morning
Tom

25/I/80
CARONA

low snow on Taos mountains
the great american conversations
how many miles from X to Y
when are we going to do the laundry
how is your car doing

15/V/80

ANOTHER POSTCARD FOR TED BERRIGAN

no I'm not going to
the silly musical event
I'm sure I'm not missing anything
though it would be very nice to meet
somebody new and interesting
forget it, too late
dear Ted
I'm going to read
Train Ride

18/X/80

from: GROSSETESTE REVIEW, VOL. 14
edited by Tim Longville, Derbyshire, England, 1981/1982

if this isn't
the gateless gate
then it is a mosquito
cruising in a Rolls Royce
up & down 10,000 BC Avenue
listening to Jimi Hendrix
Rainbow Bridge

31/3/81

fly tiny box
with the colors transfixed
dry butterfly

6/8/81
for Corrado Costa

from: COYOTE'S JOURNAL #12
edited by James Koller, Brunswick, Maine, 1988

SHE IN 24 OR MORE LINES

1.	she	of the imaginary microphone
2.	she	with the feet on the ground when needed
3.	she	slips on and off her silk stockings
4.	she	observes and reasons without rest
5.	she	reads Rabelais and Mallarmé
6.	she	makes a gift of her presence
7.	she	gives it all when she gives herself
8.	she	unprovided of reticence
9.	she	adores raspberries and blueberries
10.	she	smashes illusion
11.	she	subterranean revolution
12.	she	contemplates the great void
13.	she	finds the void everywhere
13.[a]	she	who the mirrors see
14.	she	who sees through the mirrors
14.[a]	she	travels from one place to another
14.[b]	she	registers the divers rumours
15.	she	of laconic messages
16.	she	hazards no forecasts
17.	she	wholeheartedly laughs at it all
18.	she	who deserves more than 17 lines
19.	she	who practices near-detachment
19.[a]	she	who practices detachment
20.	she	lives she breathes
20.[a]	she	who wears sex clouds and cactus
21.	she	thousand surprises in her bag
22.	she	made of nothingness
23.	she	

24.   she   who leaves tracks that are no tracks
25.   she   slips through where few can pass
26.   she   armed with objective tenderness
27.   she   broadcasts live tonight

27–28/XI/87
translated from the Italian
by the author and James Koller

from: PENINSULA, NEW WRITING FROM THE COAST
edited by Joe Safdie, Bolinas, California 1989

it's impossible to know what's poetry
    impossible to know what's poetry
it's   to know what's poetry
it's impossible   what's poetry
it's impossible to know   poetry
it's impossible to know what's poetry

10/VII/86

(temple) (bells) (wild)
(animals) (calls) (clacsons)
(Don) (Cherry) (Steve)
(Lacy) (Masahiko) (Togashi)
(only) (two) (hands)
(get) (beats) (even)
(out) (of) (wheeling)
(chair) (unison) (whistles)
(high) (higher) (thru)
(Roppongi) (dark) (bright)
(bright) (bright) (night)

14/V/86
NARITA AIRPORT, TOKYO

Shinkanzen
Bullet train
Behind sleeping
Beauty in light
Green silk dress
Roofs densely packed
Sea Rocks hills tight
Fields & forests
Go by fast

12/V/86

now I know
now I know
as far as it can go
as far as it can go

11/V/86

WANT TO BUY A ROCK?

this here thing will do
Lady Murasaki had it
directly from Genji's
latest mountain place
among the rare visits
DUE STRANE DONNE
appeared from early days
one he didn't remember
he died blind under her
very eyes   she left
with a broken heart
WANT TO BUY A ROCK?

6-7/V/86

YOSHIDA YAMA

dry creaning
dry creaming
dry screaming
dry cleaning

30/IV/86

SHIJO YANAGINOBAMBADORI

clinic & critique or
cryptic & criminal or
eat it it's typical or

30/IV/86

kanji wa jari o kansatsu shi / netsuji wa jari o nessatsu su
cold kills you with cold / heat kills you with heat

1986
Kyoto

from: GATE #4 BILL BROWN'S PARTY
*Evergreen Road Press/Bussard Journal,
edited by Franco Beltrametti & Stefan Hyner,
Bolinas, California/Rohrhof, Germany 1995*

I remember Bill Brown
fall 1967 Jim Koller introduced us in
Bolinas both were publishing Coyote's Books and
Journal, working in the Bay Area as gardeners.
I remember Bill Brown
in the light morning rain 'THE WAY TO
UNCLE SAM HOTEL' Seattle foggy and cold.
A 1966 snapshot with a hat
a redwood shingles house on the mesa
its freak stairway worried Phil's 'ON BEAR'S
HEAD' time.   San Gottardo on Columbus
"a movie in my eye".
1968 a fallen acacia across Mount Tam Driveway.
1972 "give a lady a horse and she
will get the field" (Jim loved this quote).
1974 looking for Sioux under his bed
a drawknife back to Snyder at Jack Boyce
memorial show at the Barn.
1978 the 60th birthday party at Scowley's
"a hit, talk louder" next days we didn't
make it to Point Arena where my father was born.
1987 vines and flowers all over a
downtown shack "I love Marguerite Duras, who is
Sophie Calle?"
198some a dangerous loft a broken head.
1989 in San Francisco Japantown a lunch with
Philip Whalen, "I'll get all the noodles",
"a tight fit parking", "there lives Richard
Brautigan" and later at Joanne's

"I'd smoke anything".
1992 and 1993 report letters, Bill in Taos.
1994 Bill "quietly gone" wouldve loved
the three stucco caryatid ladies
and the green one
frescoed on a walled-in window
a red rose in her left hand
opposite Arosio postoffice.
I remember Bill Brown
in light morning rain

13/XII/94 VERSION
BACK FROM MANNHEIM
typed on old Triumph with new red & black ribbon —
Riva San Vitale

from: THE DREAM NEVER BECOMES REALITY
24 Swiss Writers Challenge the United States
University Press of America, Inc., New York, 1995
edited by Cornelius Schnauber, Romey Sabalius,
Gene O. Stimpson

the moon is a lantern
hanging
through the freezing woods)
    (a Buffalo Bill show) (Hey, mister
Death, Mrs. Calamity Jane) (a super dakini
of total imagination) (a she-warrior)
sun light reflected hanging through
the freezing woods

?/XII/74

(and then) (and then) (and then) (and
then) (the wolf) (and then the wolf)
(saw) (and then the wolf saw)
(Little Red Riding Hood) (and then) (and then)
(and then) (and then) (and then)
(Little Red Riding Hood) (and then Little Red
Riding Hood) (saw) (the wolf) (and then)

5/II/77
for John Giorno

(più vecchio di Lao Tzu il para-
diso perduto) (già) (c'est la
catastrophe) (già) (do your best)
(violon) (try again) (radiateur)
(the sound of) (paradiso perduto)
(più vecchio del vecchio Lao Tzu)

23/I/77
per Steve Lacy

(people who no longer exist
guide my signs)
(people who no longer exist
dictate these words)

17/VIII/77

(plenty of light & ventilation is
important) (run, sweat, day-
dream) (do not think) (very important)
(Theodora baby blue eyes) (very, very
important) (consider clouds, water, woods,
wolves, words, BOOKLAND is a neon blue
sign) (Smith Corona, your typewriter)
(from the A-frame pitch window I see
I see I see) (where are we)

19/III/78
GEORGETOWN ISLAND, MAINE
for Joanne Kyger & James Koller

RECENT WORK
1994-1995

These poems are from Beltrametti's last manuscript partially typed, partially handwritten that contained poems in French, Italian and English. It was first published in its entirety in Gate #5, Per Franco Beltrametti, *Evergreen Road Press/Bussard Journal, Bolinas/Rohrhof 1996, and republished by Porto Dei Santi,* Loiano, Italy 2002 *with an introduction by Giulia Niccolai.*

mind wandering
in large emptiness
there isn't much
to cling to besides
coffee on stone table
distant friends letters

14/VIII/95

stumbling in the future
sneaking on Cold Motel
I saw your feet
easing in a stone house

4/VII/95
FB & KB
Mugena

when you see cows you think
cows when you hear cows you
think cows   Théodore, don't you

9/VI/95
Cold Spring in Flüelen

poetry is not a part-time job
poetry is not   part-time
poetry is not a
poetry is not
poetry is
poetry

5/VI/95

F.B. TALKS POETRY

POETRY?

In spite of and against the world kept together by repressive organization(s), the poetry we make wants to escape fixed rules. So we say, poetry doesnt offer mechanisms for solutions but exists in and belongs to this other world, the world of its reasons. Where each voice directly interrogates life without mediation.

The poets that had sound motivations not to be in struggle w/their society were the primitives — poetry was part of the whole, without having to be autonomous to exist (to resist).

For poetry a highway 2000 km long is not a highway 2000 km long — as the whole for poetry is not a *commensurate* whole, is not a whole plus its measure. "A language capable of retaining the symptoms of reality" asks the editorial of Tam Tam n.2. But what are the symptoms of reality? The canvas of poet James Koller's pick-up truck rattles in the wind.

The crudity of facts is the reality which can be realized in poetry.

Poetry: not chronicle, not only news, but in function of truth. Like for Pound, poetry is condensed language, charged w/meaning. A result projected in an intensification process. For Philip Whalen poetry is focalizing on a sheet of paper or "within yr head". Tam Tam is "barricaded" on poetry,

and has its good reasons to do it
without confusing the fact of being barricaded on
poetry w/a poetry barricaded on poetry.

Elaboration of the elaboration, not poetry
of poetry. Does poetry still exist within
yr <our> head? "On a marked rock,
following his orders, place my meat ... tempt
my new form" <Lew Welch>. But can one
really interrogate life without mediation?
Perhaps to attempt a new form of life
is not poetry?

On this order of ideas I tried with Montagna
Rossa (1971) to put together an inventory
of experiences of poetry. The symptoms of
reality are for me the poets closest to
me, they may have lived 12 centuries
ago in China, or may have disappeared
2 years ago on the mountains of the
Sierra Nevada (California) like Lew Welch,
or may live on a volcanic island like
Tetsuo Nagasawa. What they dont have in
common is much less than what they
have in common. Yet situations are
different. And different are the languages,
even irreconcilable.

What matters is the existence of people
w/antennae. How, then, these antennae
manage to transmit what they perceive, is
an internal problem of each coherence.
The coherence of Eduardo Cacciatore's poetry
for instance, in his apparent non actuality:
a freer cycle, an actuality w/a fuller

cycle. With more of a past, more of a
future.

As for the Tam Tam poets, each one in
his line of research, I see them linked
by a common keen dimension of the
text. A dimension in which the logic
of composition doesnt admit sloppiness.
Adriano Spatola's poetry need to be obsessive,
 a critically refined rhythmic insisting
verse on verse & strophe on strophe on the
thickness of language's body.
Corrado Costa moves in the infrareal w/
detached & exact words. Giulia Niccolai
explores & manipulates speeches like
unforeseen marbles of an ironic abacus.
"from the landscape of every day
experience to intellectual abstraction",
therefore.

My poetry is a synthesis of very contingent
situations, & limited — localized, pressed
"within", w/the hope of succeeding to
compress more "within", always more, a
concentrate of "spoken", or of "thought".
This is the only way I'm capable of
making poetry. I wonder if a technique
of composition is understood by the
reader as such <démasques-toi, démasquez-vous!>.

or if it is important that it is understood
as such. With the Novissimi (for instance)
composition technique is the most apparent
thing. Always comprehensible. Anyway every
game is valid. But the last dimension

of poetry is: depth. Or its charge of
evocative potential.

If anything, poetry is a barricading
in the original coherence. And not
a castle built w/the crumbs of the
dominant language. Poetry should be
practiced as a full time adventure, in
order to become itself a "symptom of
reality".

Each poem for me is a mental
(or shamanic) voyage, that can be
taken again & again. Words are resonance
boxes, perceptions, footprints, sounds.
Words & phrases have bones meat skin
tendons nerves. An interior intelligence,
almost biological. Something like an
"imitation of nature in its mode of
operation" — for Ananda Coomaraswamy, on
art as opposed to the art of practicing
sensations.

Also: poetry is high frequency communication
revealing unexpected domensions, creating
new spaces, other distances (or
proximities). Or arrows, vectors, aimed at
always new targets of white pages,
taken by surprise.

1972, DECEMBER
this copy is for Tim Longville

first published in Italian in TAMTAM N.3/4, 1973.
Translated by author & Judy Danciger.

ON POESIA DIRETTA

JK: Let's talk about *Poesia Diretta*.

FB: *Poesia Diretta* is poetry which lives basically off the page. A text becomes also a score, out of which a performance is created.

JK: Each performance is different, regardless of the fact that the same text is used?

FB: Around a strong structure one can go many directions following the given moments and conditions. Flexibility is part of it. Things alive are flexible. It also has to do with voice practices and conditions.

JK: To perform in this context is to experience performance much as one experiences writing while writing — does this imply that performance has a greater value than less complex presentations?

FB: *Poesia Diretta* I think is an open field, even more, is THE open field. It's free territory. Each poet, poet in a wide sense of course, can cut through it at different angles and bring in different research, experience, values, attitudes. Diversities don't get flattened down. Take for instance the little try we did at *Milano Poesia* in October of a simultaneous rendering of your *Fortuna Poems*, your voice in American and my voice in Italian. It built up into an unexpected vocal dimension. It provided reciprocity of invention, of context, of content. It channeled more words than usual into the given span of time. The ear can distinguish what the voice can say.

JK: One experiences more than was conceived. Conception is inadequate, doesn't extend far enough. The question of religious experience comes to mind, religion being concerned with the unknowable. Does one, by putting himself in a heightened state, in a situation where some unknown will predictably happen, attain to a variety of religious experiences? How like shamanic experience can *Poesia Diretta* be?

FB: I see it as if there were hot shamans and cold shamans. A mental poetry may shamanize through mental games and can be very tricky. A hot poetry shamanizes over 360 degrees, can be physical, elemental. People who don't see that don't see poetry as it is done these days. There is a whole spectrum. Some can play that spectrum widely, some are given to less detached choices. It's a whole free territory, no one can tell anyone what he can do or shouldn't. Though a certain global view of diversity tells a lot.

JK: I see in direct poetry simultaneous extensions of Artaud and Wittgenstein. Such performance can move totally from the realm of amusement and entertainment into the realm of involvement. At best you no longer need to sit back and speculate but rather must experience experience.

FB: This past ten years I saw poetry moving into about any field. A contamination which breaks through specialization. For instance I can't help seeing Walter Marchetti and Juan Hidalgo's performance of "Natura Morta For Grand Pianos" as *Poesia Diretta*, though words are absent and though the event is an extension of musical thought. The same for Nacho Criado's silent performance, "The Full Moon In Andalusia". I wish everybody interested could experience that. As a matter of fact, slowly and without much glamour nor publicity, poetry has penetrated into painting, into visual art, into theater, into music, into dance, and of course vice-versa, but *Poesia Diretta* can be the thread and along these lines is where it's happening. It's a wide ancient thing too. Part of it is the joy of being able to work with a few friends, poets, painter, musicians, though we all live far apart and that doesn't always facilitate the meetings and occasions. Let me name a few throughout the years, you Jim, and Corrado Costa and Tom Raworth. The painter Giovanni d'Agostino. The musicians Steve Lacy and Joelle Léandre. The dancer Valeria Magli. And you were working recently with the musician:composer Peter Garland. We don't know where we're going, but we know we're directly at it. Maybe part of the scare when poetry is directly involved comes from the very fact that the languages used are the everyday languages but in a totally different coherency that can be a shock. That's probably the permanent revolutionary aspect of it. But when something is predigested, there is no more use for it.

JK: When something is predigested, it is no longer poetry.

17/X/88
RIVA SAN VITALE
James Koller & Franco Beltrametti

IN TWO WORDS

*"The method
consists in
not following
any method.
This is
the method."*[1]

Direct poetry:
the systems
of transmitting
poetry are
directly
visible.
Concept and
practice become
extended. Everything
connected does
matter. The
image of
the canceled
arc LIVES
imaginarily in
neon. Not
everybody frequents
poetry. More
or less
everybody can
decipher pictures.
Shot from
'85 to
'92 they
reject any

unlikely inventory.
They indicate
the internal
coherences. A
possible utopia.
Like "*Our
shadows in
electric light*".[2]
An end
can change
into a
beginning. Certainly
it is
a material
already old
because we
are already
dreaming something
else, doing
something else.
From trespassing
to contamination
with disciplinary
limits, "*poetry
is something
you can
believe in*".[3]
In offering itself it
wastes itself:
a case
in point
is the
trickster-poet
survival of

differences, outside
(against) the
rule of
merchandise-form.
Against fossilization
and leveling,
for the
unexpected and
the unforeseeable,
the patient
and impatient
search is
an open
yet secret
adventure. After
throwing more
than 4000
pies,
"*nobody can
even dream
of throwing
a single
pie in
a movie*".[4]
Sure, before
an eventual
show, "*poetry
is a
place*"[5] of
meeting and
of clash.
"*It says
what it
says by*

saying it".⁶
Still life
of prepared
grandpianos with
mountains of
fruits or
electric bulbs
or words
or legs
in the
air. "*I
will only
say that
there is
eternal rebirth*".⁷
Elective meetings
are possible.
You can
break your
own bones.
A crutch
becomes an
antenna. "*Total
poetry*".⁸ beyond
the dichotomies
between life
and art,
is born
as a
score: direct
poetry is
its performance,
always different.

You can
foresee other
zones. The
directions combine
and dissolve.
The shaman
always stays
elementary. "The
metaphysical splendor
that one
must (verb)
in the poem".[9] Watch
out: nothing
must be
taken for
granted. Escaped
from the
page it
returns to
subvert it.
It can
strike as
a phallic
prank. Broken
phrases or
clichés, vivisected.
From "leave
me alone"
to "live
him alone"
to "you
know what
you left

but not
what you
will find".[10]
The tender
and violent
vortex of
"They don't
always remember":[11]
"thousands of
hours condensed
to a
few seconds".[12]
A single
bolt of
lightning: enough.
The subjective
span of
attention is
objectively short.
Beat and
beat again
"Mama mama
mama I
love you
love you".[13]
Since beyond
the given
or chosen
lineage poetry
is fatherless.
The skinned
muse tests

itself and focuses on progress in regression. It is a gamble. It is divination, *"towards which mouth goes the word river toward which voice"*.[14] It is impossible to trace borders. The text, spoken, renews itself, clarifies its own immediacy: projected density, experienced intensity. Intentional and unintentional flowing with the flow of the flow. The clues are evident. Why not repeat? Why not vary? Chance exists as

well as
the possibility
or impossibility
of all
its manipulations.
"*Impossible to
know what
poetry is*".[15]
A tribe
where you
feel-see
what you
feel-see.
The "*author's
photographical essay*".[16]
is punctual.
The day
before leaving
"*the room
is too
small. A
truck would
be better*".[17]
Invention keeps
inventing itself.

from: Antonio Ria, POESIA DIRETTA
*Mazzotta Fotografia, Milano 1992.
Translated by F.B. and James Koller*

1   Shitao, Les propos sur la peinture, Hermann, Paris 1984.
2   Tom Raworth, *Tottering State,* Paladine Books, London 1988.
3   Robert Filliou, Il Buddhismo nell'arte moderna, citando Emmett Williams.
4   Stan Laurel, *Autobiography*, New York City 1990.

5   Milli Graffi, P77 la poesia è un luogo, con G. Anceschi,
    F. Beltrametti & Pietro Gigli, In de Knipscher, Haarlem 1978.
6   Jacques Roubaud, Déduction de la forme, "Action Poétique",
    113-114, Avon 1988.
7   John Cage, Per gli uccelli, conversazioni con Daniel Charles,
    Multhipla, Milano 1977.
8   Adriano Spatola, Verso la poesia totale, Rumma, Salerno 1969
    Paravia, Torino 1978.
9   Julien Blaine, Commentaire et commendire, "Dock(k)s",
    1, nouvelle série, Ventabren 1988.
10 Nanni Balestrini, testo inedito, 1986.
11 Patrizia Vicinelli, Non sempre ricordano, Aelia Laelia,
    Reggio Emilia 1985.
12 Juan Hidalgo, Do la sol mi, "Revue d"Esthetique", 13-14-15,
    Private, Toulouse 1988.
13 Arnaud Labelle-Rojoux, Oedipe Profond, performance, 1986.
14 Corrado Costa, Il fiume, Edizione del Vicolo del Pavone,
    Piacenza 1987.
15 Franco Beltrametti, Tutto Questo, Supernova Edizioni,
    Venezia 1990.
16 Giovanni Anceschi, Come leggono i poeti, "Il Verri", 13-16,
    Mantova 1979.
17 James Koller, "Mini" Riva San Vitale 1985.

EPILOGUE

NIENT'ALTRO CHE IL VUOTO

NOTHING ELSE BUT EMPTINESS

*Pourtant je suis le premier de mon nom puisque
c'est moi qui l'ai inventé de toutes pièces*
Blaise Cendrars

Franco Beltrametti was born on October 7th, 1937, at Lago Maggiore in Ticino, Switzerland. His life would always follow the path of the wanderer that was set when he was a small child. His father, Giovanni, was an engineer for the Swiss Federal Railways, and in his early years the family moved from one railway town to the next. They finally settled in Chiasso, at the Italian border, in 1946. When his parents separated shortly thereafter, Franco moved to Lugano, where he attended the *Liceo*. As luck would have it, his French instructor was the Ticino poet Pericle Patocchi, who introduced him to Provençal poetry and to Rabelais, Verlaine, Baudelaire, and Apollinaire. Instead of textbooks he preferred reading Sartre, Camus, Villon, Ungaretti (the first book of poems he ever bought was Ungaretti's *Il Dolore*), and Pavese, and the American authors Melville and Hemingway. He took every opportunity to see the exhibitions of Lucio Fontana, Yves Klein, and Jackson Pollock in Milan, where his mother, Linda, had moved with her new husband.

In 1958 Beltrametti went to Zurich to study architecture at the *Eidgenössische Technische Hochschule*, but in 1960 interrupted his studies to take a job with an architectural firm in Paris — a move that did not stop him from continuing to explore in other directions: "nighttimes I was trying to paint, in a general Michaux plus Tobey direction"[3]. He read the Tao Te Ching and several books by D. T. Suzuki[4] and was already interested in the East Asian philosophies of Taoism and Zen Buddhism. A Chinese colleague at the architectural firm, Li Yen, helped deepen his knowledge of the basics and introduced him to the writings of the "New Americans," which at the time had rarely been translated into other European languages.

While in Paris, Beltrametti realized that the practice of architecture there was "too far from the streets and reality" for him. Despite the job's decent pay, he quit and found part-time work, spending the rest of his hours in Paris exploring ideas, meeting people, wandering the city. He started to learn English from Li in exchange for French lessons. Gregory Corso's *Happy Birthday of Death* and Jack Kerouac's *Dharma Bums* were among his readings.

In 1963 he finally finished his studies in Zurich, and by summer he'd moved to London. There he found a part-time job that allowed him to explore the city, especially the British Museum. About those days he wrote in his autobiography, "I traveled a lot, mainly to Italy, France, Spain, and Tangier. It is a mystery how I could work, study, lead a dense bar life day and night, go through girlfriends, sometimes heartlessly, read steadily, and be on the move all the time"[5]

Throughout another two years of constant rambling, he moved between Italy, France, and Switzerland, worked freelance at various building projects, and met his future wife, the American Judy Danciger. In the latter half of 1964, at the request of Li Yen and the architect Christophe Beriger, he once again returned to Zurich. There he met the painter Friedrich Kuhn and the sculptor Alberto Giacometti. He also met Urban Gwerder, with whom he would later cooperate on Gwerder's underground magazine, *HOTCHA!*, which was to be decisive in introducing the "New American Poetry" to the German-speaking audience. He soon felt another change coming. In the spring of 1965, driven by a desire to leave Europe behind, he boarded a train "to Vienna, Moscow, and the Japan of my mind"[6].

After a short stay in Moscow he journeyed on the trans-Siberian railroad to the other end of the Eurasian continent, arriving in Japan by the end of May 1965. After a few weeks spent studying Japanese and Chinese classical writing and visiting museums and the Noh theater, he met the wandering poet and "father" of the alternative movement in Japan, Nanao Sakaki, who introduced him to the American poets then living in Japan, Gary Snyder, Philip Whalen, and Cid Corman. His friendship with these poets would last his entire life and became of central importance to his literary work. There he was among like-minded poets and thinkers who took their work, and his questions, seriously. In this context he began to see himself as a poet — started to type his poems and consider their publication. Beltrametti felt most drawn to Cid Corman, who had strong ties to Europe and the European tradition.

Judy arrived in Kyoto in the fall of 1965 and gave birth to their son, Giona, in October of 1966. Not long after, Beltrametti got an offer to teach architecture at Cal Poly in San Luis Obispo, so the family decided to continue their "journey around the world." James Koller, the poet and editor of *Coyote's Journal*, met their ship at the San Francisco harbor in the spring of 1967. He would become one of Beltrametti's closest friends, and for the next three decades they took innumerable reading tours in the US and across Europe. In the months after their meeting, Koller introduced Beltrametti to a series of other American poets, among them Joanne Kyger, Lew Welch, Michael McClure, and Allen Ginsberg, and to the painter Jack Boyce, the sculptor Jack Augsburger, and the gardener and prose writer Bill Brown, a close friend of Charles Olson. At that time, too, the San Francisco Bay Area was the poetry center of the US. What started with the now-legendary reading at the *Six Gallery* in San Francisco on October 6th, 1955 reached a climax with the *Berkeley Poetry Conference* in the Summer of 1965. Daily life was permeated by poetry; the poet, no longer dwelling in an ivory tower, took an active part in shaping daily realities. Social interaction was an important component of art; publication turned public. Poetry was understood as an oral tradition and a formative element of society. This insight became fundamental in Beltrametti's art, and he would remain faithful to it for the rest of his life.

After a journey across the North American continent, he returned to Zurich in the summer of 1968. During that period, he attended a series of lectures by Krishnamurti with his old friend Christophe Beriger in the Bernese town Saanen. From Ticino, where he turned down an offer to cooperate on the design of the Chiasso-San Gotthard highway, he traveled via Milan to Rome. In Milan Beltrametti got to know the translator Fernanda Pivano, a meeting that prompted his translations of texts by William Burroughs, Richard Brautigan, Joanne Kyger, and James Koller for the anthology *L'Altra America*.

The sojourn in Rome was where Beltrametti became "part of the Italian avant-garde poetry scene"[7]. While working on his novel *Nadamas* he met, in quick succession, the poets Nanni Balestrini, Giulia Niccolai, and Adriano Spatola. Spatola was so taken by Beltrametti's poetry that he decided to publish the manuscript *Uno di quella gente condor*, in the series *geiger*, which he'd been publishing for Feltrinelli in Milan.

In the fall of 1969 he, Judy, and Giona traveled to Partanna, Sicily, where they lived for the next year among the people who had lost their homes and possessions in the great earthquake of 1968. He worked with the group *Centro Studi e Iniziative della Valle del Belice* trying to organize cooperatives for the reconstruction, but the constant political infighting of the various groups became too much for him. His report about the time there, *Belice lo stato fuorilegge*, was published by Feltrinelli. The family moved on to Venice. Here he met Ezra Pound, who by that time had lapsed into complete silence. "I felt respect for the fragile old man; we never got beyond eye contact"[8]. But the family couldn't find a home in Venice, so they moved on and spend the winter of 1970-71 in a small vacation cottage above Lugano, which "proved to be the right place to get very depressed, entangled in knots of my own making."[9] He wrote a key poem:

> My demons
> I see coming out
> even from where
> I thought them exorcised
> they say they're feeling well
> we're getting to be friends

In the spring of 1971 a friend from his adolescent years, the architect Flora Ruchat, offered Beltrametti an apartment in her house in the Swiss town Riva San Vitale, near Mendrisio — from then on he would always maintain a residence there. After a journey to California, Beltrametti returned to Europe in the early summer of 1972 and edited several issues of the magazine *Tam Tam*, which Spatola was publishing. At that time he also translated, with Judy's help, Jaime de Angulo's *Indian Tales* into Italian. Later in the year an opportunity appeared to buy a piece of property in California near Gary Snyder and Allen Ginsberg. After some prolonged back and forth with the US Immigration Office, he got his green card in the spring of 1974. At the same time, he and Judy started to live separately.

After he'd acquired some basic knowledge about carpentry by helping build Snyder's barn, Beltrametti constructed a house based on his own design and lived there until the beginning of winter. He wrote extensively about this time in his second novel, *Quarantuno,* and in the collection of poems titled *California Totem*. He then returned to Europe and visited Judy and Giona in a small village in the Ardèche, France.

At the end of 1975 he met the French action artist and poet Julien Blaine at a book fair in Le Havre. He'd planned to fly back to California from Luxembourg afterward, but on the night before departure, while driving with Marcello Angioni and Giovanni Blumer, he was seriously injured in a car accident. During the three months spent in the hospital there, a project evolved for an international poetry magazine, *Abracadabra,* in collaboration with Udo Breger and Dutch poet Harry Hoogstraten, that would go on to publish five issues. When he was released from the hospital his right foot was still seriously damaged, and it wasn't until after several months of therapy, toward the end of 1976, that he could walk without crutches. In April of 1977 he held the first exhibition of his paintings at the renowned art gallery *Ziegler* in Zurich. In the meantime, James Koller arrived in Switzerland and, together with Harry Hoogstraten, they toured for several weeks through Europe. During a stroll through the English Garden in Munich Beltrametti had the idea of a poetry festival called *P77*. The project was met with enthusiasm from his poet friends, so the first festival took place in Venice in September 1977. It was the beginning of a series of festivals that took place in Amsterdam, Paris, Milan, and Tarascon over the next several years.

During a reading tour through the US with Hoogstraten and Koller in the spring of 1978, Beltrametti got to know Ted Berrigan, a central figure of the New York scene, and Ed Dorn, a poet and former student of Charles Olson. In New York he also met Annabel Levitt, who published his *Airmail Postcards;* together they translated Blaise Cendrars into English. At the poetry festival *P78,* which took place in Amsterdam in the fall of that year, Beltrametti met the British poet and performance artist Tom Raworth, with whom he would go on to collaborate on countless performances and publication right up to his last days. The festival *P79* in Amsterdam was such a success that the following festivals there became commercialized, and Beltrametti refused to have anything to do with them.

During the 1980s, neoliberalism's increasing influence resulted in a cuts in government incentives for the arts. It didn't take long until this was felt among the small press avant-garde, which up to that point never had to make commercial success its major concern. During a US reading tour with Jim Koller in 1980, Beltrametti formed the slogan: "Another day, another dollar LESS."[10] About these times Beltrametti wrote in his autobiography: "Life through the eighties wasn't an easy ride. I kept learning the hard way how to survive without going out of my concerns. It takes obstinacy, integrity, and discipline: money made with poetry and art is rare and you can't buy poetry grocery, no, you've got to buy grocery grocery. But since the almost-deadly car crash in Luxemburg 1975, I feel that I'm just going on the ways indicated by my dead friends and teachers. Make it new, give what you know and learn what you don't."[11]

But by the end of the 80s Beltrametti's perseverance had begun to pay off, and a number of his works were being published in different countries. He traveled to Kyoto in 1986, where he attended the opening of an exhibition of his paintings: twenty years later he returns to the place that had such a lasting impact on his life as an artist. The year after, he toured again with Koller with their program *Graffiti Lyriques*, documented in the book by the same name. He organized a poetry festival in Riva San Vitale and started publishing his small magazine *Mini*. 1989 saw the formation of the *Gang of Four*: Franco Beltrametti, Julien Blaine, James Koller, and Tom Raworth. Their performances were a combination of word and image created spontaneously on the stage. They toured with that program through the US and Europe.

In 1990, Supernova in Venice published *Tutto Questo*, a comprehensive selection of Beltrametti's writings from 1977 to 1988, which was republished in French four years later with the additional years 1989-1991. Between 1991 and 1995 he held numerous exhibitions in France, Italy, and Switzerland. His artwork sold well, and for the first time in many years no financial pressure weighed on him. During that time some of his most beautiful books were published: *Monte Generoso, 13 portraits de trobairitz*, and that true treasure of typography *Regina Di*. In 1994 Beltrametti met the Ticino potter Antonella Tomaino; they lived together from then on.

Toward the end of that year he started working on the project *Choses qui voyagent*, the first complete retrospective of all his work, to include artwork as well as writing, with exhibitions and readings planned in Venice, Milan, Marseilles, and Paris for 1995 and 1996. The exhibition catalog shows Beltrametti's unique status as a multilingual writer-artist who moved seamlessly between image and word. The catalog was published shortly before his unexpected death on August 26, 1995.

Franco Beltrametti was a wanderer among worlds — many worlds, the "real" ones as well as those imagined — but never the world of the marketplace. He was an archeologist of the mind; even his home in Ticino seemed like a camp, and he was constantly at the point of departure or just passing through. Like Blaise Cendrars, one of his earliest models, he took the Trans-Siberian Railroad to the other end of the Eurasian continent. From there he took a step further and went to Japan, a culture that had a significant influence on him through Buddhism, ever present in Kyoto, and through the friendships with Cid Corman, Gary Snyder, and Philip

Whalen. Perhaps it was Whalen's statement from the 1959 "Since You Ask Me" that had the most persistent effect on Beltrametti's own work:

> *This poetry is a picture or a graph of a mind moving, which is a world body being here and now which is history...and you. Or think about the Wilson Cloud-chamber, not ideogram, not poetic beauty: bald-faced didacticism moving as Dr. Johnson commands all poetry should, from the particular to the general.*[12]

Beltrametti's main concern was to accurately "graph" this constant movement, but to avoid theory while doing so, since the reflection involved tends to bring movement to a standstill. Thus the question of *quality* or even *sense* had no role in his work, since these are merely phenomena of reflection. Still, he had a high level of aesthetic creativity and recognized early on the irrelevance of "effort"; this is one reason his work seems so nimble-footed. In this respect he was similar to the early practitioners of Chinese art, who were influenced by the tradition of Ch'an Buddhism. It comes as no surprise that one of Beltrametti's few writings about poetry starts with a quote from Shih T'ao's "Talks on Painting":

> The method consists
> in not having a method.
> That is the method.[13]

Beltrametti went from Japan to California in 1967 in search of the roots of his own family: his grandfather Guiseppe had owned a dairy farm in Mendocino County around 1900. In the 1960s, alternatives to the "American Way of Life" dominated all things, and by extension, the literary scene. He became an intermediary between this other America and the European avant-garde, a role that reached its high point with the festivals he organized in Venice and Amsterdam during the second half of the 70s.

Despite this close connection to the US, Beltrametti was essentially a European poet and remained independent from popular movements. While poetry in the US slid gradually into the dungeons of the academy, the "family of poets," the *tribe* as he called it, was always most important to him. When, during the 80s, the so-called "Naropa Poetry Wars" split the North American scene into two camps, he made a great effort to bridge this gap and bring people together again.

Although Beltrametti might be seen as an important but little-known figure of the (Southern) European avant-garde, his influence on the American literary scene is more than marginal. He didn't have the egocentric character necessary to attract fame from the public. Many of his early works are lost — he even destroyed some himself — in his travels, both physical and artistic. But during the years following his death his name has come up in many places and connections. He left, even among the younger generation who never knew him personally, a gentle trace — just as it suited his character, gentle and lasting, not troubled by short-lived sensation. And so it seems the right time to make his English work available to the reader again.

Beltrametti cared about poetry in all its diversity, never for dogmatic demarcations and exclusions. He never gave anything but all — that was for him the only possibility; it was his natural way. That in this process, just as in nature, not everything would survive goes without saying, but this diversity was to Franco Beltrametti always an expression of the "great general," the all-encompassing emptiness, from which everything arises.

Stefan Hyner

EMPTY-BOAT STUDIO
MONTH OF THE POMEGRANATE
YEAR OF THE WOODEN-GOAT 2015

---

1 *Nothing else but emptiness*, a recurring motto in Beltrametti's work.
2 "However, I'm the first one with my name since I'm the one who made it [all] up." From Blaise Cendrars, *Complete Poems*. Ron Padgett, translator. 1993, University of California Press.

3   Franco Beltrametti, "1937—" in *Contemporary Authors, Autobiography Series,* Volume 13, 1991. Gale Research Inc., Michigan.
4   Ibid.
5   Ibid.
6   Ibid.
7   Ibid.
8   Ibid.
9   Ibid.
10   Ibid.
11   Ibid.
12   Philip Whalen, *On Bear's Head.* 1969, Harcourt, Brace & World, Inc. and Coyote.
13   Franco Beltrametti, *Poesia diretta: In due parole*, Milano, Mazotta 1992. Original quote from *Shitao, Les propos sur la peinture*, Paris 1984.

BIBLIOGRAPHY

Uno di quella gente condor, Torino, edizioni geiger 1970

Nadamas, Torino, edizioni geiger 1971

Un altro terremoto, edizioni geiger 1972

Face to Face, Pensett, Staffordshire, Grosseteste Review Books 1973

One of those condor people, Brunswick Maine, Blackberry Books 1974

Truck Tracks, (w/Joanne Kyger) Bolinas, California, Mesa Press 1974

Note sul condor, Tremona, Caos Press 1975

In transito, Torino, edizioni geiger 1976

Quarantuno, Racconto in 41 capitoli annotati, Roma/Milano, Cooperativa Scrittori Romanzi/AR&A 1977

Oog in Oog, Haarlem, in de Knipscheer, 1977

Andiamo, (w/Harry Hoogstraten & James Koller) Fort Kent, Maine, Great Raven Press 1978

Trattamento micologico del mondo, (w/Marcello Angioni) Melano, Caos Press 1978

Airmail Postcards, New York City, vehicle editions 1979

El Tibetano en ander proza, Haarlem, in de Knipscheer, 1981

Target, Wirksworth, Derbyshire/Leeds, Yorkshire, Grosseteste Books 1981

E allora, (poesia 1977-81) Mulino di Bazzano, Parma, Tam Tam 1982

Il libro delle X, Salorino/Riva San Vitale, Nana Press & Scorribanda Productions 1983

1984, Mulino di Bazzano, Parma, Tam Tam 1984

Mail, (w/Tom Raworth) Riva San Vitale [?], Scorribanda Productions, 1984

Banana Story, eccetera, Caneggio, Stamperia della Fronteria 1985

(past) (present) (future), Bath, Maine, Coyote's Journal 1986

19 permutazioni, Venezia, Edizioni Inedite 1986

The Thoughts of Captain Alexis, (w/ *Tom Raworth*) Cambridge/Riva San Vitale, Infolio & Scorribanda Productions 1987

Surprise, Brunswick, Maine, Coyote's Journal 1987

Perché muoiono i nanetti sconosciuti, (w/ *Tom Raworth*) Cambridge/Riva San Vitale, Infolio & Scorribanda Productions 1987

Graffiti Lyriques, (w/James Koller, Dario Villa & Julien Blaine), Milano, avida dollars 1988

Nado nado, Ventabren [?], Zérosscopiz Nèpe 1988 [?]

A Gang of 4, (w/*Julien Blaine, James Koller & Tom Raworth*) Brunswick, Maine, Coyote's Journal 1989

Niente da, Milano, Corpo 10 1990

Tutto Questo, Venezia, Supernova Edizioni 1990

Monte Generoso, Mendrisio, Ascona Presse 1991

Dossier Villon, (w/*Corrado Costa*) Reggio Emilia, edizioni Elytra 1991

Franco Beltrametti 1937- 10.000 words autobiography, Contemporary Authors. Autobiography Series, volume 13, Detroit/London, Gale Research Inc. 1991

13 portraits de trobairitz, Ajaccio, Akenaton editions 1991

Clandestin, Marseille, CIPM /Spectres Familiers 1991

Poesia diretta (w/*Antonio Ria*) Milano, Mazzota 1991

KTCFYW (w/*Tom Raworth*) Riva San Vitale/Cambridge, Scorribanda Productions & Infolio 1992

Trattato nanetto, Venezia, Supernova Edizioni 1992

Three for Nado, Weymouth, Dorset, Stingy Artist/Last Last Straw Press 1992

Regina di, Locarno, l'impressione edizioni 1991

Logiche & Illogiche, Riva San Vitale, Giona Editions 1994

Tout ça, Saint-Etienne-Vallée-Française, AIOU 1994

Perché A, Venezia, Supernova Edizioni 1995

CHOSES QUI VOYAGENT. <<QUAND ON AIME IL FAUT PARTIR>>, Milano, Mazotta 1995

ONZE TAKES PLUS UNE, Riva San Vitale/Saint-Etienne-Vallée-Française, Giona Editions & AIOU 1995

UCCELLO BLU VOLA, Chiasso, Edizioni Tettamanti 1996

ANTO CE MATIN, Rouen, derrière la Salle de bains 1996

THE POSSIBLE MOVIE (*w/James Koller*), Brattleboro, Vermont/ Saint-Etienne-Vallée-Française, coyotaiou 1997

RECENT WORK, Gate, A Poetry Magazine, Rohrhof/Bolinas, Gate & Evergreen Road Press 1996 [2nd edition: Porto dei Santi, Loiano, gnams edizioni artigianali numerate 2002]

READ & SEE THE RED SEA, Rohrhof, Gate 1999 [2nd edition: Brunswick, Maine, Coyote 2006]

CALIFORNIA TOTEM, Berlin, Stadtlichter Presse 2002

I TEND TO SIMPLIFY EVERYTHING, Green River, Vermont, Longhouse 2004

NADAMAS, Berlin, Stadtlichter Presse, 2004

ZWEITER TRAUM, Secondo sogno, Zürich, Limmat, 2014

Die Veröffentlichung dieses Buches wurde ermöglicht durch
die freundliche Unterstützung des Cantons Ticino,
der Gemeinde Riva San Vitale,
der Fondazione Franco Beltrametti
sowie der Kulturstiftung Pro Helvetia.

The publication of this book was made possible
by the generous financial support of:
the Canton Ticino
the Municipality Riva San Vitale
the Fondazione Franco Beltrametti
and the Swiss cultural foundation Pro Helvetia

swiss arts council
prohelvetia

Letters, manuscripts and other materials about F.B.
can be found at the Swiss National Archives at
www.nb.admin.ch/aktuelles/03147/03950/04232/index.html?lang=de